Alfred Russel Wallace

Titles in the series Critical Lives present the work of leading cultural figures of the modern period. Each book explores the life of the artist, writer, philosopher or architect in question and relates it to their major works.

In the same series

Alfred Russel Wallace

Patrick Armstrong

REAKTION BOOKS

In memory of Robert Thomas Keegan,
a fine scholar and an inspiring teacher, 1952–2017

Published by Reaktion Books Ltd
Unit 32, Waterside
44–48 Wharf Road
London N1 7UX, UK

www.reaktionbooks.co.uk

First published 2019
Copyright © Patrick Armstrong 2019

Printed and bound in Great Britain by Bell & Bain, Glasgow

A catalogue record for this book is available from the British Library

ISBN 978 1 78914 085 9

Contents

Abbreviations

The following abbreviations have been used for quotations in the text from Wallace's principal works.

CCD   *The Correspondence of Charles Darwin* (Cambridge, 1985–)

Life   *My Life: A Record of Events and Opinions*, 2 vols (London, 1905)
           For *Life* vols I and II, the abbreviation is followed by the volume and page number

MA   *The Malay Archipelago: The Land of the Orang-utan and the Bird of Paradise. A Narrative of Travel with Studies of Man and Nature* (London, 1869). There have been many editions of this work, and so the chapter is indicated, not the page. A very useful recent edition is *The Annotated Malay Archipelago*, ed. J. van Wyhe (Singapore, 2015)

W. Cent. *The Wonderful Century: Its Successes and Its Failures* (London, 1898)

Narrative *Narrative of Travels on the Amazon and Rio Negro: With an Account of the Native Tribes, and Observations on the Climate, Geology, and Natural History of the Amazon Valley* (London, 1853; 2nd edn 1889)

World of Life *The World of Life: A Manifestation of Creative Power, Directive Mind and Ultimate Purpose* (London, 1910)

Access to most of Wallace's publications, and much other material, is available at 'Wallace Online', see http://wallace-online.org

Preface

Alfred Russel Wallace was the joint discoverer, with Charles Darwin, of evolution through natural selection. But while Darwin's name is immediately recognized, fewer people remember the part that Wallace played.

One biography of Wallace was entitled *Darwin's Moon*, implying that perhaps he rotated around Darwin, or was eclipsed by him. Another, more recent, *In Darwin's Shadow*, seems to be saying that he was completely overshadowed by Darwin. This is unfortunate, as Wallace had in some ways the more interesting life. He was, without doubt, Darwin's superior in terms of eccentricity and was probably more active in a greater number of fields.

Wallace's contribution was enormous. He wrote some 22 books and approaching 1,000 articles and other publications. He was a political activist and controversialist in a way that Darwin never was – even allowing for the hornets' nest that the latter's *On the Origin of Species* stirred up in the years after its publication in 1859. Wallace lived to a great age, from the first quarter of the nineteenth century until the eve of the First World War. It is entirely appropriate that he be considered in his own right.

Darwin had advantages: he came from a well-to-do family and was educated at Shrewsbury School, Edinburgh Medical School and Christ's College, Cambridge. He was at the centre of things at the same time as Wallace was wandering round the group of islands that is now Indonesia. Darwin's *On the Origin of Species* had been twenty years in the making and set the agenda for evolutionary debate for the next century, whereas no single work by Wallace had anything like the same impact, although *Darwinism* (1889), titled as a tribute to his colleague, and *The World of Life* (1910) were significant summaries in their time.

Alfred Russel Wallace rose to eminence through his own efforts, without the advantages of class, background and education. At one stage he described himself in his youth as 'a very dull, ignorant and ill-educated person', but later he was certainly the opposite of all these things. And matters would have been very different were it not for Wallace's letter to Darwin in June 1858, and the speedy, and much-debated, decision of colleagues Charles Lyell and Joseph Dalton Hooker to put a joint presentation – consisting of Wallace's paper plus a couple of statements of Darwin's ideas – before the Linnean Society a few weeks later. Without this, the world might have had to wait years for the doctrine of evolution through natural selection. The world would have been very different.

This book attempts, occasionally, to make comparisons between these two intellectual giants of nineteenth-century science. However, the aim is, first and foremost, to provide – in a compact form – the essential facts of the life and work of Alfred Russel Wallace, and to show he was a many-sided, complex character, to which the title 'The Great Victorian Polymath' is appropriately given.

Alfred Russel Wallace in 1902.

1

Early Life

The life of Alfred Russel Wallace can be seen, on one level, as a story of an individual's triumph over difficulty, tragedy and hardship, as well as anxiety and uncertainty.

Oddly, the theme of uncertainty touches even his very origins. For much of his life, Wallace believed that he had been born in 1822. However, very late in life he came across an old prayer book, in which had been written down Alfred's date of birth, together with those of all of his siblings – in Alfred's father's handwriting. (It was the custom of the day to record the main events of family history in the flyleaves of a Bible or prayer book, and until the passing of the Births and Deaths Registration Act of 1836, such entries were often taken as evidence for the date of a birth or death, or of age.) The entries clearly showed that he was born on 8 January 1823, and that he was baptized just under six weeks later, on 16 February. It must have been gratifying, as he approached his eighties, for Alfred Wallace to discover that he was younger than he thought.

As regards the other circumstances of his birth, there is little doubt. He was born at Kensington Cottage – the name is a slight misnomer; it is rather more than a cottage – in the tiny village of Llanbadoc, across the river from the small town of Usk, in the old Welsh county of Monmouthshire. His parents were Thomas Vere Wallace and Mary Anne Wallace (née Greenell), a middle-class English couple of relatively modest means. He was the eighth of nine children;[1] three of his siblings did not survive into adulthood.

Wallace's birthplace, Kensington Cottage, near Usk, Monmouthshire, Wales, from his autobiography *My Life* (1905).

Wallace's father was of Scottish descent (allegedly from a lineage going back to the Scottish hero William Wallace), while the Greenells were a respectable family from Hertford, to the north of London.

His account of the house, from his autobiography, bespeaks a happy early childhood:

> I clearly remember the little house . . . with a French window opening to the garden, a steep wooded bank on the right, the road, river, and distant low hills to the left. The house itself was built close under this bank, which was quite rocky in places . . .
>
> The river in front of the house was the Usk, a fine stream on which we often saw men fishing in coracles, the ancient form of boat made of strong wicker-work, somewhat the shape of the deeper half of a cockle-shell, and covered with bullock's hide . . . But the chief attraction of the river to us children was the opportunity it afforded for catching small fish, especially lampreys (*Life*, I, 20–21).

Wallace thought that these recollections must have gone back to when he was about four years old. It seems that from his very early years he was a good observer of the world about him.

There is another incident from this early period that perhaps provides a glimpse of the practical, scientific approach that characterized his later work. Aesop's *Fables* were often read to him, and he remembered the tale of the thirsty fox that found a vessel with a little water in the bottom, but with an opening too small for its snout. In the fable the fox dropped stones into the vessel, making the water rise to the point that he could reach it. The young Alfred attempted an experiment to replicate this. He dropped pebbles into a mug containing a couple of centimetres of water. But the soft gravel from the path contained finer, silty material, and to the youngster's acute disappointment, the water turned into mud. The young Wallace regarded the experiment as a failure, but the incident perhaps provides an early example of self-instruction in the experimental method, of careful observation by an autodidact, and also of a literalist interpretation of something he was told.

A number of Alfred Wallace's relations, on both sides, were lawyers, and his father had qualified in law and had worked briefly as a solicitor. But Thomas Wallace soon forsook the law for business. He attempted tutoring, publishing a magazine devoted to art and antiquities, property speculation and running a subscription library – all were failures; he had no aptitude for business, and seems to have been rather gullible. According to his son, at times as a young bachelor Thomas Wallace 'lived idly' and 'enjoyed himself in London . . . as a fairly well-to-do, middle class gentleman', sometimes taking in the season in Bath (*Life*, 1, 7–10). Almost inevitably, he and his family eventually fell on tough economic times. The move to Wales was probably an attempt to relocate to somewhere they could live more cheaply.

Sometime in 1828 the family moved from Usk to Hertford, Mrs Wallace's home town. Once there, the family shifted from house to house frequently, and misfortunes continued; Mr Wallace was again swindled. Thus it was that, as Alfred Wallace himself put it, 'The children who reached their majority had little or nothing to start with in earning their living, except a very ordinary education' (*Life*, I, 14). Mr Wallace had attempted for the most part to teach his children at home.

However, for a few years Alfred went to Hertford Grammar School. This seems to have been a somewhat Dickensian establishment (the building dated from 1617), and Alfred described the head, a Mr Crutwell, as 'irascible'. The schoolroom was badly lit, and the pupils had to bring candle-ends, which they stuffed into old ink-pots. Discipline seems to have been rather ragged. The boys were flogged with a cane from time to time by the head, and one of the other masters used to rap the boys' knuckles with a ruler until they were 'black, swollen and had the skin cut'. Latin, particularly the translation of Virgil's *Aeneid*, and some of the writings of Cicero, was emphasized, as it so often was in those times. Possibly because of further financial difficulties in the family, Alfred left the school before starting Greek. Alfred recalled that 'next to Latin grammar the most painful subject I learnt was geography', which he stated consisted of learning by heart lists of towns, provinces and rivers – it was indescribably boring (*Life*, I, 54).

No doubt because of the family's continuing impecuniousness, in his final year school fees were reduced on condition that he assist with the teaching. He found his position as an intermediate creature, somewhere between teacher and pupil, very disagreeable and uncomfortable.

Just as when he was a very young child in Wales, Alfred seems to have found the lessons to be learned from the Hertfordshire countryside more worthwhile than those indoors involving Latin, geography or mathematics. He appears to have wandered at will – a bit of a loner perhaps – through what he recalled late in life to be an idyllic landscape of coppices and hedgerows, old manor houses and watermills. As a growing lad, he wondered about the chalk that seemed to be everywhere below the surface, and from which springs bubbled here and there. He climbed some of the 'stumpy yew trees' and noticed different types of wild flowers in the damp, stream-side meadows of the Lea Valley.

He left the school just after his fourteenth birthday, in March 1837 – not Christmas 1836 as he claimed in his 1905 autobiography, *My Life* (Wallace's published dates are more than occasionally incorrect). Fourteen was the normal school-leaving age at the time. Shortly after, he was sent to live with a Mr Webster in Robert Street, Hampstead Road, London, where his elder brother, John, was apprenticed. Mr Webster was a small-scale master-builder and his workshop manufactured doors, staircases, floorboards and other joinery for the houses that he built. Some eight or ten men were employed, and hours of work were from 6 a.m. to 5.30 p.m., with an hour and a half for meals. Wallace wrote that the few months he spent here 'at the most impressionable age had some influence in moulding my character, and also furnished me with information which I could have obtained in no other way' (*Life*, 79), although he does not say much about why this was so. One can, however, make certain deductions. The title of Chapter Six in *My Life* gives a clue: 'London Workers, Secularists and Owenites'. Although small jobs were occasionally found for him, he had little else to do other than watch the men work and listen to their conversation. Despite their uncertainties and anxieties, home and grammar school had been relatively protected environments. Here in London the young Wallace mixed with the true working class, and heard the occasional lewdness of speech. He came to know how much each man earned and thus understood something of the men's difficulties and aspirations, so becoming equipped to argue about changes in the costs and standards of living of the working class from a position of real factual knowledge. In later life, with his somewhat socialist, leftish or radical views, he was to do exactly that.

The other important influence at this time was his regular attendance at the 'Hall of Science':

> It was really a kind of club or mechanics' institute for advanced thinkers among workmen, and especially for the followers of Robert Owen,[2] the founder of the socialist movement in England. Here we sometimes heard lectures on Owen's doctrines, or on the principles of secularism or agnosticism, as it is now called; at other times we read papers or books, or played draughts, dominoes or bagatelle, and coffee was supplied to any who wished for it. It was here that I first made acquaintance with Owen's writings, and especially with the wonderful and beneficent work he had carried on for many years at New Lanark. I also received my first knowledge of the arguments of sceptics, and read amongst other books Paine's *Age of Reason* (*Life*, I, 87).

One assumes that in a 'Hall of Science' there were occasional lectures on science itself, but Wallace says relatively little about these in his writings. What he got, above all, from this establishment in Tottenham Court Road, and in what he *read* there, was the idea that established views were to be *questioned*.

Indeed, in meeting and conversing with ordinary working men, in reading the works of Thomas Paine and Owen, Wallace was finding the questioning tone of voice that ran through so much of his later work. This is to be found in his writings on social, economic and political themes; in his strange ideas on spiritualism; and in his belief in the pseudosciences of mesmerism and phrenology, as well as in his considerations of the possibility of the miraculous, and the speculations on the fixity of species for which he is best remembered.

There are a couple of further points that might be made here. Intrinsic to the doctrines of Owenism and of socialism that were circulating at this time was the notion of 'improvement', the idea that under the type of socialism that Owen espoused, the social and moral character of humanity might be improved. And discussion of Thomas Malthus and his ideas was also not unusual in Owenite circles at the time – the *Essay on the Principle of Population* had been published in 1798. Just possibly, we can see vague echoes of these teenage discussions of *directionality*, and an appreciation of the importance of 'checks' to population growth, in Wallace's later evolutionary thinking.

But the stimulations of London were destined to be short-lived. In the summer of 1837, at just fourteen-and-a-half years of age, Wallace went with his elder brother William to Bedfordshire, over 32 kilometres (20 mi.) northwest of Hertford, to begin his training as a land-surveyor. The Tithe Commutation Act of 1836 had just come into effect, and the parishes of much of England were surveyed as part of the procedure for the consolidation of tithes. Tithes were an ancient right of the Church of England to one-tenth of all produce, and the act of 1836 converted this clumsy procedure into a money payment. (This payment was itself abolished by another statute in 1936.)

There was thus a great deal of work for land-surveyors, and the two brothers took up residence at an inn at the village of Barton-le-Clay, north of Luton. It was here that young Alfred became interested in geology. His brother had some interest in the subject, and he showed the younger lad fossil oysters of the genus *Gryphaea* and belemnites (which Alfred had thitherto called 'thunderbolts'), both of which were common in the deposits around Barton.[3]

Alfred learnt the basics of surveying and mapping, and the technique of calculating the areas on a map by using trigonometry. At the same time, he supplemented this work by reading an account, belonging to his brother, of the Trigonometrical Survey of England and Wales, conducted from 1784 to 1796. This book contained details of all the observation stations on hilltops, church towers and other conspicuous features, the angles between them and the calculated lengths of the sides of the triangles that united them.[4] Two nearby churches had been used as observation points in the earlier survey, and the line joining them ran across the parish the brothers had to map; they made it their chief baseline, and the young Alfred was pleased to find that their measurements coincided closely with those made by the Trigonometrical Survey. He had a pocket sextant, and its regular use opened his mind to the practical applications of mathematics, about which he had been taught 'nothing whatever' at school.

Alfred read eagerly about all the surveying instruments used and the precision with which measurements were made. He noted the importance of the accurate measurement of baselines by means of steel chains, and of the necessity for adjustments to be made for temperature, a factor which could cause contraction and expansion of the chains. He read of the manner in which the surveyors measured the baseline in two directions, and then worked from major triangles down to lesser. Throughout his life, he loved and admired detail, particularly fine, oft-repeated scientific detail.

Reading about these matters, while attempting to put some of the principles into practice each day that he was engaged in the Tithe Apportionment Survey, must have been an excellent, systematic training. It would have shown Alfred the importance of precision in maintaining records and in making repeated observations, as well as the advantages of benefiting from the accumulated knowledge and experience of others.

Moving around the Bedfordshire countryside seems to have reawakened his interest in natural history, latent in his psyche following his wanderings in Monmouthshire and in the Lea Valley countryside in early childhood. He began to want to know the names of the wild flowers, shrubs and trees that he met with in his daily work.

Surprisingly, after two active summers of survey work, which he clearly enjoyed, Alfred spent a few months working for a clock- and watch-maker in Leighton Buzzard, Bedfordshire. The Mr Matthews who ran the business did some other types of engineering and survey work; perhaps he also dealt with surveying instruments as well as clocks, or perhaps there was a temporary reduction in the amount of survey work available. Recalling the period later, Wallace remarked that the short period in this employment taught him he would never succeed in business: he said in his autobiography that felt he was 'not fitted by nature for such a career'. He was almost certainly right.

Alfred found work in the office and workshop extremely dull, and in the autumn of 1839, aged sixteen-and-a-half, he travelled with his brother William to Kington in Herefordshire – not far from the countryside of his early childhood – and the two of them undertook surveying projects on either side of the Welsh border over the next couple of years. Again, the young Alfred Wallace enjoyed the outdoor work; when he was just seventeen, he wrote to a childhood friend,

It is delightful on a fine summer's day to be . . . cutting about all over the country . . . following the chain and admiring the beauties of nature, breathing in the fresh and pure air on the hills, or in the noontime heat enjoying our lunch of bread and cheese in a pleasant valley by the side of a rippling brook (*Life*, I, 143).

This rejoicing in the outdoor world, and in hard physical work, was to characterize much of his later life. In addition, the years in the Welsh borderlands – Herefordshire and Radnorshire, and a little later to the southwest at Neath, Glamorgan, while he was living in Wales itself – also consolidated themes from earlier stages in his life. For example, he had described the Hall of Science he visited in London as 'a kind of mechanics' institute', although at the time about which he was writing, the mechanics' institute movement had not got fully underway. However, the movement spread rapidly through the Welsh Borders in the 1830s and '40s: institutes were established at Rhayader in 1839, Hereford in 1840 and Hay-on-Wye, Builth Wells and Kington in 1841.[5]

Alfred Wallace seems to have been a keen member of the Kington Mechanics' Hall from its commencement. Despite his membership seemingly lasting just a few months (because he moved to Neath late in 1841), one of the first papers presented at Kington's Hall was given by one 'Mr A. Wallace, a member of the Institute'. It was titled 'An Essay on the Best Method of Conducting Kington Mechanic's [sic] Institution'.[6] The eighteen-year-old's first paragraph was as follows:

> Mechanics' Institutions are societies which of late years have been established in many towns in the kingdom, for the purpose of applying the principle of combination in affording scientific instruction to all persons, and especially the working classes. They are distinguished from Literary and Philosophical Societies, principally by attempting to diffuse information on the various branches of practical science, and those that relate to the mechanical and other arts.

He listed the books that he felt should be placed in the Institute's library, including Charles Lyell's *Principles of Geology*, as well as Roderick Murchison's *Silurian System* – Silurian rocks underlie parts of Shropshire and central Wales. *The Penny Magazine* and *Magazine of Science* were 'too trifling'; he preferred the annual reports of the British Association for the Advancement of Science.

His own enquiries into geology continued. In his autobiography he refers to 'an isolated craggy hill called Stanner Rocks', which being of a 'very hard kind of basalt very good for road-metal, was continually being cut away for that purpose'.[7] He describes how, on one occasion, he went some distance out of his way to inspect a waterfall, noting the rock surface 'formed by the regular weathering of slaty beds in fine layers'. In the summer of 1841 he surveyed in the Brecon Beacons, and noticed the flat, tabular summits of some of the mountains.

On one occasion, at about this time, a 'tall Irishman' who worked in the same office gave an evening talk 'on human nature'. In his recollection of the event, Wallace was very critical: the lecture, he recalled,

> consisted of a rather prosy exposition of the ideas of Aristotle and the mediaeval schoolmen on human physiology, without the least conception of the science of the subject at the time he was speaking (*Life*, 1, 142).

He was clearly quite at home with the idea of a scientific presentation, followed by discussion, questioning and criticism. In his Kington essay he stressed the importance of every member of the Institute presenting a paper or introducing a discussion.

In Wallace's description of his sojourns in Kington and Radnorshire, he gives an account of what he perceives as the evils of the enclosure movement. Phrases such as 'cruel robbery', 'families reduced from comfort to penury', 'the old have been driven to the workhouse', 'cottagers . . . had no compensation whatever' and 'legalized robbery of the poor for the aggrandisement of the rich' appear. It seems that he did not write about these matters at the time, or participate in any political activities: perhaps as a trainee land-surveyor he was too close to the landed gentry for it to have been wise of him to loudly voice his opinions.

But he does seem to have thought about such matters. The questioning continued.

The period of residence in and near Neath was divided into two phases: a period with his brother William from 1841 until the end of 1843, and another in 1846 and 1847 with another brother, John (after William's death). The stay was broken by a period schoolmastering in Leicester, when it became apparent that there was insufficient land-surveying business to support both Alfred and William. In many ways, themes that can be identified in Alfred's earlier development can be seen as continuing. These include a zeal for self-education, wide reading, the constant relating of theoretical study to the practical, a questioning approach, an enthusiasm for collecting, naming and classification (to an almost obsessive degree), the giving and attending of lectures at mechanics' halls and elsewhere, and the organization of his thoughts into sustained writing.

There are varied instances that illustrate these traits of Wallace's. For example, having learned the use of the sextant in surveying, and because his brother had a book on nautical astronomy as well as Hannay and Dietrichsen's *Almanack*,[8] he 'practised a few of the simpler observations', including 'finding the latitude' from the altitude of the Sun and the stars. He also made a telescope to observe the Moon and Jupiter's satellites. As usual, he attempted to relate his reading to practical activities, while the development of his enthusiasm for naming, and particularly for *order* and classification, continued. In 1841 (that is, at the age of eighteen), Wallace obtained a cheap paperback published by the Society for the Diffusion of Useful Knowledge giving an outline of the structure of plants and

> also a good description of about a dozen of the most common natural orders of British plants. Among these were the Cruciferae, Caryophylleae, Leguminosae . . . This little

book was a revelation to me, and for a year was my constant companion. On Sundays I would stroll in the fields and woods, learning the various parts and organs of any flowers I could gather, and then trying to find how many of them belonged to any of the orders in my book. Great was my delight when I found that I could identify a Crucifer, an Umbellifer, and a Labiate; and as one after another the different orders were recognised, I began to realize for the first time the order that underlay all the variety of nature (*Life*, I, 192).

Sometimes he realized that the plants he found were members of orders that were not described in his book. Other volumes were purchased from his meagre allowance or borrowed, and by carefully comparing the plants he found with the various reference sources at his disposal, he set to work 'with increased ardour to make out the species of all the plants' he could find.

But I soon found that by merely identifying the plants I found in my walks I lost much time in gathering the same species several times, and even then not always being quite sure I had found the same plant as before. I therefore began to form a herbarium, collecting good specimens and drying them between drying papers and a couple of boards weighted with books or stones . . . [I] used then to take long walks over the mountains with my collecting box, which I brought home full of treasures (*Life*, I, 195).

Always he demonstrated the zeal for order, organization and classification, a desire for detail and the linking of theoretical study with practical application.

As mentioned, for a while there was insufficient work for both William and Alfred in the surveying business, and so shortly after Alfred's twenty-first birthday, in January 1844, William told his younger brother that he must make his own way in the world. Alfred briefly attempted to find employment in London, but then applied for work as a teacher at the Collegiate School in Leicester. Rather surprisingly, in view of the truncated and somewhat disorganized nature of his own education, he was successful. He was to teach English, drawing, geometry and mapping for 'about thirty or forty pounds a year'. One advantage of this appointment was that there was a good library in Leicester, from which Wallace was able to obtain books that were to prove of great significance to him: Alexander von Humboldt's account of travels in South America, Malthus' essay on population and also *Vestiges of the Natural History of Creation*, a work of speculative natural history and philosophy with an evolutionary theme, published anonymously in 1844.[9] Another advantage was that it brought him into contact with the naturalist Henry Walter Bates (1825–1892), a member of the local mechanics' institute, with whom he later went to South America.

Wallace saw Bates's collection of insects – butterflies and beetles – and learned of the enormous variety of beetles that were to be found within a few miles of Leicester. The focus of his interests shifted from plants to beetles: 'I at once determined to begin collecting . . . I therefore obtained a collecting bottle, pins and a store-box in order to learn their names and classification' – there was that love of collecting, classification and the search for order once again.

Alfred's father had died in 1843, and William, the brother who had taught him surveying in the fields and hills of Wales and the Welsh borderlands, quite suddenly followed him, from pneumonia, in early 1846.[10] Alfred and another brother, John (with whom he had worked in London), travelled to Wales to deal with William's affairs and collect outstanding debts. By this time, the railway-building boom was under way, and the two of them were able to carry on the surveying business until late in 1847, as the proposed routes of the railways across the land had to be identified and mapped.

Henry Walter Bates, Wallace's companion in South America, in later life.

By the later 1840s, Neath and nearby Swansea were significant centres. A Literary and Philosophical Society had been founded in Neath in 1834 and the Mechanics' Institute in 1843. Wallace served as curator to the Museum of the Neath Philosophical and Literary Institution (that love of order again) and lectured in physics at the

Mechanics' Institute (for which Alfred and John had drawn up plans, and with which Alfred continued to be associated). He had the use of a good library at the Philosophical and Literary Institution, which by 1842 held the books that he had earlier recommended for Kington.

Wallace's first literary effort – that on the Kington Institute – written at the age of eighteen in 1841, was followed by several more letters or short pieces published, or at least prepared, in the 1840s. All were significant, illustrating aspects of his interests and character that were already developed and presaging themes from his life and work that were yet to come. One piece, which does not seem to have been published at the time, was the text for a proposed lecture on plant classification. In it, he discussed the concept of classification in general, arguing that 'any classification is better than none'. (The talk is summarized in Chapter Fourteen of volume I of *My Life*.) He stressed the advantages of a 'natural' classification. Linnaeus's classification, making use of a few well-marked and easily observed characters, and allocating generic and specific names, as binomials, was an advance on what had gone before. Looking back on these early efforts late in life, Wallace commented,

> Its chief interest to me now, is that it shows my early bent towards classification, not the highly elaborate type that seeks to divide and subdivide under different headings with technical names, rendering the whole scheme difficult to comprehend . . . but a simple and intelligible classification which recognises and defines all great natural groups, and does not needlessly multiply them on account of minute technical differences (*Life*, I, 200).

A classification, he thought, should be an aid to learning and understanding, not an aim in itself, and he thought that the arrangement of the natural orders of flowering plants provided the best example of such a system.

The second unpublished piece was 'The Advantages of a Varied Knowledge' – not surprising for one who was already something of a jack of all trades, and who developed into one of the Victorian era's greatest polymaths. (The essay is also summarized in *My Life*.) 'The South-Wales Farmer: His Modes of Agriculture, Domestic Life, Customs and Character' was Wallace's third piece. This account has something of an ecological flavour, describing the Welsh countryman against the background of the valleys and mountains that formed his home. One section, reflecting its author's interest in botany, was a description of a hillside plant community in which Wallace listed the species found, giving their scientific names. Although unpublished at the time, Wallace was evidently rather proud of this account, as it is reproduced almost in full in volume 1 of *My Life*.

His first real scientific publication came a little later: it was a one-sentence reply to a correspondent of *The Zoologist*, who regretted that no specimen of a particular species of beetle had been collected for twenty years:

> Capture of Trichius fasciatus near Neath. – I took a single specimen of this beautiful insect on a blossom of Carduus heterophyllus [melancholy thistle] near the falls at the top of Neath Vale – Alfred R. Wallace, Neath.[11]

Within months of this note appearing in 1847, he had made the decision to travel to South America with Henry Bates. In 1850 Wallace's first substantial scientific paper – 'On the Umbrella Bird' – was published in the *Proceedings of the Zoological Society of London*. In view of the time taken for mail to travel from South America, it may have been written late in 1849. Some ten papers and two books appeared over the next five years. Alfred Russel Wallace's formative period was over.

During his first twenty years of life, Wallace had shown a remarkable ability to overcome obstacles. His father and several siblings had died, including a brother to whom he was close. He had moved house frequently. His formal education had been cut short, perhaps partly though his father's impecuniousness. He had only actually been employed for a short time at the school in Leicester and for the few months with a clock-maker in Leighton Buzzard. The businesses with which he had been associated, between brief periods of success, had had periods of difficulty. But he had learned enough – in the fields and hills of the Welsh Borders, from his brother, at mechanics' institutes and in public libraries. He had learned the principles of surveying and map-making, picked up the rudiments of science and discovered how to take his place among other scientists and present information orally and in writing. His brief time in London had made him politically aware and developed in him a questioning approach. The foundations had been laid.[12]

2

South American Journey

Having been robbed of much of his formal education, Alfred Russel Wallace became an autodidact: it is possible that having his schooldays reduced, and never having been to university, gave him a certain independence of mind, a characteristic that manifested itself both in his thirst for travel and adventure and his ability to generate new ideas. And possibly the variety of different occupations he had pursued over the first two decades of his life provided him with a certain flexibility and an ability to cope with different situations. There is even a tale illustrating that the few months working with a watch-maker proved useful: once on his travels he needed to calculate tides and was able to take a watch to pieces, clean it and reassemble it.

The young Wallace read widely, using the resources of public libraries and mechanics' institutes whenever he could. Malthus's essay on population, Darwin's *Voyage of the Beagle*, Lyell's *Principles of Geology* and Robert Chambers's anonymously published evolution tract *Vestiges of the Natural History of Creation* were devoured during his early adulthood in Leicester and Neath. He was persuaded to lecture on science at the Mechanics' Institute in Neath.

As mentioned in Chapter One, while teaching in Leicester he encountered the youthful entomologist Henry Bates, who had published a paper on beetles in the *Zoologist* while still a teenager. They corresponded about the books they were reading and the insects that they were by then both collecting. Of particular influence was a volume by the American William Henry Edwards, first published in 1847 and titled *A Voyage up the River Amazon, Including a Residency at Pará*. This is, in places, somewhat extravagantly written, describing how 'the thousand shades of green were enamelled with flowers, in red, white and gold.' Edwards noted that

> Around the tree-trunks clasp those curious anomalies, parasitic plants, sometimes throwing down long slender shoots to the ground, but generally deriving sustenance from the tree itself and from the air . . . These are in vast numbers of every form . . . Often a dozen varieties cluster on a single tree. Towards the close of the rainy season they are in blossom, and their exquisite appearance as they encircle the mossy and leafy trunk with flowers of every hue can scarcely be imagined. At this period vast numbers of trees add their tribute of beauty, and the flower-domed forest from its many-coloured altars ever sends heavenward worshipful incense. Monkeys are frolicking through festooned bowers, or chasing in revelry over the wood arches. Squirrels scamper in ecstasy from limb to limb, unable to contain themselves for joyousness . . . Birds of the gaudiest plumage flit through the trees . . .[1]

Who could resist the charms of such a place?

Inspired by the accounts of earlier travelling naturalists such as Edwards, but also including Alexander von Humboldt and Charles Darwin, Wallace decided that he too wanted to travel to the tropics as a naturalist. Influenced by *Vestiges of the Natural History of Creation*, he also hoped to gather evidence for the transmutation of species. In 1847 Wallace wrote to Bates:

> I begin to feel rather dissatisfied with a mere local collection – little is to be learnt by it. I sh[d] like to take some one family, to

study thoroughly – principally with a view to the theory of the origin of species.[2]

The *Vestiges* clearly had a strong impact on Wallace. In later life, he recalled that

> I well remember the excitement caused by the publication of *Vestiges* and the eagerness and delight with which I read it. Although I saw that it really offered no explanation of the process of change of species, yet the view that change was effected, not through any unimaginable process, but through the known laws and processes of reproduction commended itself to me as perfectly satisfactory, and as affording a first step towards a complete and explanatory theory (*W. Cent.*, 138).

In a letter of 9 November 1847 to Bates, he asked him whether he had read the work. Bates was obviously somewhat critical in his reply, for in a later letter (28 December) Wallace comments,

> I have a rather more favourable opinion of the 'Vestiges' than you appear to have. I do not consider it a hasty generalization, but rather an ingenious hypothesis supported by some interesting facts and analogies, but which remains to be proved by more facts and the additional light which more research may throw on the problem . . . It furnishes a subject for every observer of nature to attend to . . . and it thus serves both as an incitement to the collection of facts, and an object to which they can be applied when collected (*Life*, I, 254).[3]

Wallace, if not also Bates, thus had a clear, if very incomplete, conceptual framework in his mind before departing for South America. In part at least, the expedition had the objective of collecting evidence for the development of an evolutionary approach to understanding the diversity of nature. (We may note in passing that Charles Darwin had no such formulation in his mind when he embarked on HMS *Beagle* in late 1831.)

Much of the latter part of 1847 and early 1848 must have been spent on a busy round of collecting the materials they needed, and learning how to use them. Wallace and Bates met a Mr Edward Doubleday, an authority on insects at the British Museum (at that time the natural history collections had not been separated off from those of art and archaeology), who advised them that much of Brazil 'was very little known' and that collecting insects, shells, mammals and birds from there for sale to museums and collectors would allow them to 'easily . . . pay expenses'. They also met with Edwards, the author of *A Voyage up the River Amazon*, and obtained an open letter of introduction. A Dr Thomas Horsfield of the India Museum, a rather strange cabinet of curiosities in Leadenhall Street, instructed them in how to pack materials in boxes for transport, and they secured an agent, Samuel Stevens. Proprietor of the Natural History Agency in Bloomsbury Street, close to the British Museum, Stevens undertook to receive and submit for sale the specimens they forwarded to him.

Thus on 28 April 1848 Alfred Russel Wallace and Henry Bates embarked at Liverpool on the *Mischief*, a vessel of 192 tons, bound for Brazil. In his autobiography, Wallace deals with the voyage succinctly but quite descriptively:

> We were told that she was ranked A1 at Lloyds, and that we might therefore be quite sure that she was thoroughly seaworthy. We were the only passengers, and were to have our meals with the captain and mate, both youngish men . . . Soon after we got out to sea the wind rose and increased to a gale in the Bay of Biscay, with waves that flooded our decks, washed away part of our bulwarks, and was very near swamping us altogether. All this time I was in my berth prostrate with sea-sickness, and it was

'A. R. Wallace in 1848', from *My Life* (1905).

only, I think, on the sixth day, when the weather had become fine and the sea smooth, that I was able to go on deck just as we had a distant sight of Madeira. Shortly afterwards we got into the region of the trade-wind, and had fine, bright weather all the rest of the voyage. We passed through part of the celebrated Sargasso Sea, where the surface is covered with long stretches of floating

Henry Walter Bates having an 'Adventure with curl-crested toucans', illustration from his *The Naturalist on the River Amazons* (1863). After shooting and wounding one individual of this spectacular species, Bates says he was mobbed by a whole group. (Some authors have maintained that the image resembles Wallace rather than Bates!)

sea-weed, not brought there by storms from the distant shore, but living and growing where it is found, and supporting great numbers of small fish, crabs, mollusca, and innumerable low forms of marine life. And when we left this behind us, the exquisite blue of the water by day and the vivid phosphorescence often seen at night were a constant delight, while our little barque, with every sail set, and going steadily along day and night about ten knots an hour, was itself a thing of beauty and a perpetual enjoyment (*Life*, 1, 267–8).

The two men arrived at Pará (now Belém in Pará state) a month after leaving Liverpool. Bates and Wallace were aged 23 and 25 respectively, full of the enthusiasm (and naivety) of youth, and a tinge of disappointment colours some of Wallace's earliest annotations on the place: the public buildings were in poor repair, even 'ruinous'. The town as a whole was 'a curious outlandish-looking place'. On his first walk into the nearby forest he expected to see 'monkeys as plentiful as at the Zoological Gardens, with hummingbirds and parrots in profusion'; however, for some days he did 'not see a single monkey and hardly a bird of any kind'.

Their intention was to fund their expedition by collecting insects and other animal specimens in the rainforests of the Amazon and selling them to private collectors and museums in the United Kingdom and Europe. In time they 'got their eyes in' and marvelled at the many different species of palm tree close to where they lived; before very long Wallace and Bates had accumulated four hundred species of butterflies, as well as hosts of beetles and other insects.

For the first few months the two worked together as a team, but before long they had a disagreement, possibly over some trivial matter, and split up to collect in different regions, although they met from time to time to discuss their work. Bates moved towards the Andes, while Wallace collected from the middle Amazon region and the Rio Negro area, making notes on the peoples and languages he encountered as well as on the geography, flora and fauna. He drafted a map of the region using some of the skills he had learned as a land-surveyor in the Welsh Borders and described his methods in his characteristically detailed way:

> During the two ascents and descents of the Rio Negro and Uaupés in 1850–1852 I took observations with a prismatic compass, not only of the course of the canoe, but also of every visible point, hill, house, or channel between the islands, so as to be able to map this little-known river. For the distances I timed our journey by a good watch, and estimated the rate of travel up or down the river, and whether paddling or sailing. With my sextant I determined several latitudes by altitudes of the sun, or of some of the fixed stars. The longitudes of Barra and of San Carlos, near the mouth of the Cassiquiare, had been determined by previous travellers, and my aim was to give a tolerable idea of the course and width of the river between these points, and to map the almost unknown river Uaupés for the first four hundred miles of its course (*Life*, I, 316).

From these observations he made a large map to illustrate a paper which he read before the Royal Geographical Society in 1853. A version of the map was published with the paper; it contained much information as to the nature of the country along the banks of the rivers, such as the isolated granite mountains and peaks and some of the cataracts that Wallace ascended, together with information on some of the native tribes that inhabit the region. The map was sufficiently accurate for it to become the standard map of the area for decades.

Wallace had the knack of being able to convey, elegantly but with scientific accuracy, the nature of an environment. Here he is describing the ecological structure, and the biodiversity, of the virgin tropical forest: it was

> everywhere grand, often beautiful and even sublime. Its wonderful variety with a more general uniformity never palled. Standing under one of its great buttressed trees – itself a marvel of nature – and looking carefully around, noting the various columnar trunks rising like lofty pillars, one soon perceives that hardly two of these are alike. The shape of the trunks, their colour and texture, the nature of their bark, their mode of branching and the character of the foliage far overhead, or of the fruits or flowers lying on the ground, have an individuality which shows that they are all distinct species differing from one another as our oak, elm, beech, ash, lime, and sycamore differ. This extraordinary variety of the species is a general though not universal characteristic of tropical forests, but seems to be nowhere so marked a feature as in the great forest regions which encircle the globe for a few degrees on each side of the equator. An equatorial forest is a kind of natural arboretum where specimens of an immense number of species are brought together by nature.
>
> . . .
>
> [A] second feature, that I can never think of without delight, is the wonderful variety and exquisite beauty of the butterflies and birds, a variety and charm which grow upon one month after month and year after year, as ever new and beautiful, strange and even mysterious, forms are continually met with (*Life*, I, 287–8).

Although he does not use the term, or anything like it, he clearly understands the notion of *biodiversity* – the number of species or organisms per unit area. In this, as in so much else, he was ahead of his time.

'Interior of primæval forest on the Amazons', illustration from Bates, *The Naturalist on the River Amazons* (1863).

But as well as seeing 'the big picture', Wallace had an excellent eye for detail. Here he is describing a single species of organism:

[The] Umbrella Bird . . . is in size and general appearance like a short-legged crow, being black with metallic blue tints on the outer margins of the feathers. Its special peculiarity is its wonderful crest. This is formed of a quantity of slender straight feathers, which grow on the contractile skin of the top of the head. The shafts of these feathers are white, with a tufted plume at the end, which is glossy blue and almost hair-like. When the bird is flying or feeding the crest is laid back, forming a compact white mass sloping a little upward, with the terminal plumes forming a tuft behind; but when at rest the bird expands the crest, which then forms an elongated dome of a fine, glossy, deep blue colour, extending beyond the beak, and thus completely masking the head. This dome is about five inches long by four or four and a half inches wide. Another almost equally remarkable feature is a long cylindrical plume of feathers descending from the lower part of the neck. These feathers grow on a fleshy tube as thick as a goose-quill, and about an inch and a half long. They are large and overlap each other, with margins of a fine metallic blue. The whole skin of the neck is very loose and extensible, and when the crest is expanded the neck is inflated, and the cylindrical neck-ornament hangs down in front of it. The effect of these two strange appendages when the bird is at rest and the head turned backwards must be to form an irregular ovate black mass with neither legs, beak, nor eyes visible, so as to be quite unlike any living thing. It may thus be a protection against arboreal carnivora, owls, etc. . . . The umbrella bird inhabits the lofty forests of the islands of the lower Rio Negro, and some portions of the flooded forests of the Upper Amazon (*Life*, I, 314–15).

A short paper, 'On the Umbrella Bird', was sent back to Britain and published in 1850.[4]

'An umbrella bird with its wonderful crest', illustration from Bates, *The Naturalist on the River Amazons* (1863).

Wallace's accounts of his explorations over the next few years are full of references to difficulties and obstructions overcome, adventure, danger and derring-do. Problems included the desertion of the assistants that he had retained to help him; risks posed by rapids, whirlpools and waterfalls on the rivers they were traversing by canoe; being harassed by ants and other insects; attacks by vampire bats; and fear of jaguars and snakes, as well as the 'heat of the equatorial sun', when the temperature was allegedly up to '95° [F or 35°C] in the shade'. But the trials of exploring this exotic land were more than compensated for by the excitements of collecting: 'The more I see of the country, the more I want to, and I can see no end of the species of butterflies when the country is well explored,' he wrote.[5]

They lived off the land, eating ants as well as turtle and caiman meat. Wallace records wandering through the forest one morning, hearing a rustling in the branches above and seeing a large monkey looking down at him. The following day he saw a whole troop of monkeys in the same area. One was shot, and Wallace reports that 'the poor little animal was not quite dead, and its cries, its innocent looking countenance and delicate little hands were quite childlike.' The creature was cooked and eaten and the meat was described as 'resembling rabbit' (*Narrative*, 42).

Wallace is making a comparison here between the anatomy and behaviour of primates with humans. Darwin made similar comparisons: from his days on the *Beagle* he made important observations on the behaviour of organisms, as well as their morphology.

Wallace in fact made a special study of the monkeys with which he came into contact: in his years in the Amazon Valley, he observed 23 species. As well as their appearance and behaviour, he was at pains to note their distribution. Even at this early stage, the one who was to become known as 'The Father of Biogeography' was arranging his material around themes that were to be important later. In an article written up for London's Zoological Society, Wallace made a 'few remarks' on the distribution of the various species of monkey that he saw; he deplored the vagueness and inaccuracy of location labels attached to specimens describing the places where previous naturalists had collected them, and he grumbled that 'there is scarcely an animal whose exact geographical limits we can mark out on the map.' He went on:

> On this accurate determination of an animal's range many interesting questions depend. Are very closely allied species ever separated by a wide interval of country? What physical features determine the boundaries of species and of genera? Do the isothermal lines ever accurately bound the range of species, or are they altogether independent of them? What are the circumstances which render certain rivers and certain mountain ranges the limits of numerous species, while others are not? None of these questions can be satisfactorily answered till we have the range of numerous species accurately determined.[6]

During his time in the Amazon forests he thus took every opportunity of determining the geographical limits of species, and he found

> that the Amazon, the Rio Negro and the Madeira formed the limits beyond which certain species never passed. The native hunters are perfectly acquainted with this fact, and always cross over the river when they want to procure particular animals, which are found even on the river's bank on one side, but never by any chance on the other. On approaching the sources of the rivers they cease to be a boundary, and most of the species are found on both sides of them.[7]

This analysis was published within weeks of his return to England, while his memories of the South American forests were still very clear; he must have been thinking about distributions and boundaries, and their implications, while he collected and explored. Perhaps his days surveying and map-making in Bedfordshire and the Welsh borderlands encouraged him to think in terms of boundary lines and spatial patterns.

Such observations are entirely compatible with Wallace's future ideas on evolution, even though he does not spell out his later argument in these early writings. Species isolation, effected by a river or mountain range, may be followed by variation and change in the original population, so that genetic differences accumulate. Closely related species are thus sometimes found almost adjacent to each other – they were once part of the same population.

It was not just the distribution of vertebrates that fascinated Wallace. Another of his early papers was 'On the Habits of the Butterflies of the Amazon Valley' – showing that he understood the subtle interplay of habitat, habits (behaviour) and appearance. Again he comments on the effect of isolation and boundaries. He noticed, for example, that 'The *Callitheas* are another genus of butterflies unsurpassed for exquisite beauty. The *C. Sapphira* inhabits the south bank of the Lower Amazon, while immediately opposite to it is found an allied species, the *C. Leprieurii*.' And as with butterflies, he was intrigued with trees, monkeys, fish and a host of other groups: he was impressed by the enormous number of species in any area.[8]

It will be clear from the above that Wallace and Bates had aspirations to research the 'species question', and indeed they had had a vaguely evolutionary agenda at the outset of their journeys in South America. It seems that Wallace was making tantalizing sallies in evolution's direction: he was beginning to understand the importance of isolation and the role of boundaries separating taxa; he was experimenting with ideas linking environment, morphology and behaviour; and he noticed the diversity of species per unit area in the rainforest. But he was not quite there.

Interestingly, some of his comments that come closest to later evolutionary views are made in a rather surprising setting. Propagating liberal, even socialist, views in later life, Wallace had, from his very early adulthood, definite views on race, and in particular the subjection of one race to another – he did not like slavery. He saw it on the estate of a Señor Calistro in June 1849. He later recorded his thoughts: 'Can it be right to keep a number of our fellow creatures in a state of adult infancy, of unthinking childhood?' he enquired, continuing,

> It is the responsibility and self-dependence of manhood that calls forth the highest powers and energies of our race. It is the struggle for existence, the 'battle of life', which exercises the moral faculties and calls forth the latent sparks of genius. The hope of gain, the love of power, the desire of fame and approbation, excite to noble deeds, and call into action all those faculties which are the distinctive attributes of man (*Narrative*, 121).

The notion of the 'struggle for existence' or 'battle of life' was of course a key component in the concept of evolution by natural selection, embraced years later by both Wallace and Darwin.

In 1849 Bates and Wallace were briefly joined by the young explorer-botanist Richard Spruce, and then by Wallace's younger brother Herbert, who had found it difficult to settle in a job in England, and on hearing of Alfred's success in collecting, resolved to try his hand. Herbert was something of a versifier and captured the experience of travelling by boat along the river through the forest quite perceptively:

> And now upon the Amazon,
> The waters rush and roar—

The noble river that flows between
A league from shore to shore;
Our little bark speeds gallantly,
The porpoise, rising, blows,
The gull darts downward rapidly
At a fish beneath our bows,
The far-off roar of the onça,
The cry of the whip-poor-will—
All breathe to us in whispers
That we are in Brazil
(*Life*, 1, 278).

('Porpoise' = Amazon River dolphin, *Inia geoffrensis*;
'onça' = jaguar, *Panthera onca*.)

But Herbert did not seem to have much enthusiasm for natural-history collecting and returned to Pará before very long, dying of yellow fever on 8 June 1851, aged 22, before he could return to England. Alfred was away up country collecting and exploring and could not be with him. He was devastated. Tragedy seems to have stalked poor Alfred Wallace through much of his early life.

Alfred's health deteriorated, too, and on 12 July 1852 he embarked for England on the brig *Helen*. He noted that he was 'still suffering from fever and ague', which had come close to killing him ten months before on the upper Rio Negro, and from which he had never been free since. The *Helen* had a mixed cargo of rubber, cocoa, annatto (a yellow dye and flavouring derived from the seeds of the achiote tree, *Bixa orellana*), piassaba (the woody fibres from a species of palm, formerly used for making brooms) and 'balsam of capivi' (a resin, traditionally used in medicine, from another tropical tree, copaiba, *Copaifera officinalis*) – along with dozens of cases containing Wallace's specimens and many of his notes.

However, after 26 days at sea, 1,126 km (700 mi.) off the island of Bermuda, the ship's cargo caught fire and the entire crew was forced

THE BRIG "HELEN" ON FIRE.

O 2

The brig *Helen* on fire, 6 August 1852, illustration from William Henry Kington, *Shipwrecks and Disasters at Sea* (1875).

to abandon ship. Wallace's account, taken from a letter he later wrote to the *Zoologist*, says it all:

> On the 6th of August, when in lat. 30° 30'N., long. 52°W., at 9, a.m., smoke was discovered issuing from the hatchways, on opening which, and attempting to ascertain the seat of the fire, the smoke became more dense and suffocating, and soon filled the cabin, so as to render it very difficult to get any necessaries out of it. By great exertions the boats were got out, and bread, water, and other necessaries put into them. By noon the flames had burst into the cabin and on deck, and we were driven to take refuge in the boats, which, being much shrunk by exposure to the sun, required all our exertions to keep them from filling with water. The flames spread most rapidly; and by night the masts had fallen, and the deck and cargo was one fierce mass of flame.[9]

It was the capivi balsam, a resinous, volatile substance, that had caused the destruction. Normally, small kegs of the balsam were stored in wet sand, and some was stowed in this way. However, just before departure another boatload of balsam had been brought alongside for transportation and as there was no sand to use as packing, rice chaff – a highly flammable substance – had been used instead. It seems as though the fire was an accident waiting to happen.

All of the specimens Wallace had with him were lost. He could only save a part of his diary and a few sketches. Wallace and the crew spent ten days in a leaking, open boat before being picked up by the brig *Jordeson*, which was sailing from the Caribbean to London. The *Jordeson*'s provisions were much strained by the extra passengers, and the ship itself was deficient in a number of respects and nearly foundered, but after a difficult passage on very meagre rations, the ship finally reached Britain on 1 October 1852: the return voyage had taken eighty days.

After his return to the UK, Wallace spent eighteen months in London living largely on the insurance payment for his lost collection – his agent had had the foresight to insure the specimens, although for less than their value – and from selling a few specimens that had been shipped back earlier during his sojourn in South America. During this period, despite having lost almost all of the notes from his expedition, he wrote six scientific papers and two books – *Palm Trees of the Amazon and Their Uses*, an early work in what subsequently became ethnobotany, and *Travels on the Amazon*. He established links with a number of British naturalists, including Charles Darwin, with whom he had a few minutes' conversation in the Insect Room of the British Museum.[10]

3

Eight Years in Southeast Asia

After the tragedy of the fire at sea, Wallace arrived in England, with, almost literally, nothing but his shirt to his name. Fortunately for him, his agent and broker, Samuel Stevens, took things in hand. The returned traveller was taken to an outfitter, and a suit was bought for him. In due course his agent also helped him find accommodation (although for a time Wallace lived with his mother). Stevens had taken it upon himself to insure the cargo of specimens, and £200 (the equivalent of well over £20,000 in 2018), on which Wallace was able to live for some months. Despite the devastating effect, from a scientific point of view, of losing nearly all of his specimens and most of his notes, Wallace seemed able to recover remarkably quickly.

He used the next eighteen months very efficiently. A naive, self-educated youth on his departure, he was almost immediately accepted into scientific circles on his return. In this he resembled Darwin, who was hobnobbing with the leading naturalists of the day within weeks of the return of the *Beagle* – but then Darwin had the head-start of being a Cambridge man, and *he* had his specimens. Between his return from the Amazon and early 1854 Wallace published papers in the *Annals and Magazine of Natural History*, the *Proceedings of the Zoological Society of London*, the *Zoologist*, the *Transactions of the Entomological Society of London* and the *Journal of the Royal Geographical Society*. In most of these cases, publication followed the presentation of the paper as a lecture delivered at a meeting of the respective society. His paper on the butterflies of the Amazon Valley was perhaps particularly prescient. It was read before the Entomological Society on 7 November and 5 December 1853, and almost as a throwaway it contains the following remarks:

> The most characteristic of the Amazon valley are those species of *Heliconia* with white or yellow spots on a shining blue or black ground, such as the *Antiocha*, *Thamar*, and several others; those with radiating red lines on the lower wings, such as *Erythræa*, *Egeria*, *Doris*, and several undescribed species; and, lastly, the delicate little clear wings of the genera *Thyridia*, *Ithomia* and *Sais*. All these groups are exceedingly productive in closely allied species and varieties of the most interesting description, and often having a very limited range; and as there is every reason to believe that the banks of the lower Amazon are among the most recently formed parts of South America, we may fairly regard those insects, which are peculiar to that district, as among the youngest of species, the latest in the long series of modifications which the forms of animal life have undergone.[1]

Wallace here speaks as an experienced collector and observer, and the level of detail is excellent. Although the ideas are incomplete and imperfect, we already see the idea that organisms change over time, and a relationship between present distributions and 'the long series of modifications' that had occurred over time is hinted at. Some biological groups are assumed to be more 'productive' of new forms than others. Also of interest is the fact that Wallace was already comparing his observations with those of Darwin, and that this comparison was in respect of the behaviour of insects:

> We now come to a group of insects peculiar to America, the *Ageronidæ*, and in them we first see a deviation from the normal

Transition forms between Heliconius Melpomene and H. Thelxiope.

s 2

'Transition forms' of butterflies 'between *Heliconius melpomene* and *H. thelxiope*', from Bates, *Naturalist on the River Amazons* (1863).

manner of carrying the wings in repose; the species of this family invariably resting with the wings expanded. Five species are found about Pará, and they all frequent dry situations, and always settle on trunks of trees, with the head downwards. The singular noise produced by these insects has been noticed by Lacordaire and Mr Darwin. The common species, *A. Feronia*, produces it remarkably loud, when two insects are chasing each other and constantly striking together.[2]

Even if they did not know one another well personally, Wallace was well aware of Darwin's early work – he had of course read the *Voyage* before he departed for South America. And both were supremely interested in the *behaviour* of organisms. As well as meeting Darwin (in the Insect Room at the British Museum), he gave a talk at a Linnean Society meeting on palms. Wallace also heard Thomas Huxley (later known by some as 'Darwin's Bulldog')

T. H. Huxley, in an engraving after a drawing by T. B. Wirgman, *c.* 1882.

Wallace in 1853, from his autobiography, *My Life: A Record of Events and Opinions* (1905).

lecture, in December 1852; he was impressed by the manner in which Huxley seemed able to make a 'difficult and rather complex subject perfectly intelligible' (*Life*, I, 323).

As before and subsequently, Wallace had difficulty in securing reliable salaried employment and, despite the rigours of his South American adventures, must have felt a certain restlessness. He thought about an expedition to East Africa; Australia was considered; he spent a short time in France and Switzerland. Wallace also exploited his connection with the Royal Geographical Society, having recently 'had the honour to lay before the Society ... his map and description of the Rio Negro'. Managing to get the president of the RGS, Sir Roderick Murchison, on his side, he was fortunate in securing some funding from the Society, and decided, after some vacillation, on what was then called the Malay Archipelago for his next collecting venture. A plan emerged for him to be carried to the Far East on one of Her Majesty's naval vessels, and Wallace spent some fourteen days aboard HMS *Frolic*, a 16-gun, 511-ton sloop. But the Crimean War was in prospect, and the ship was needed elsewhere for transport – and so Wallace disembarked.[3]

Eventually the slow-grinding mills of the RGS, the Foreign Office and the Admiralty did their work, and with Sir Roderick helping things along, official support for Wallace's scientific expedition was forthcoming, in the form of a ticket on a P&O ship to Singapore. Wallace took with him a London boy, Charles Allan, as an assistant, stating that his young helper was sixteen although he looked younger – he was actually fourteen.

He seems to have been adequately, but not lavishly, equipped. There is a list of equipment in the back of one of his notebooks:

2 double barrel guns
1 single barrel gun
1 Colt revolver
15 lb [7 kg] [gun]powder
6 bags of shot Nos 2 to 10
4,000 caps
A bag of bullets
Arsenic, pepper and alum 10 lbs [4.5 kg] [for treating skins]
2 bag nets, 1 wasp [net?] & 1 moth forceps
2 drying boxes
Camphor [to repel insects from specimens]
2 axes
2 jungle knives[4]

Wallace must also have taken with him a number of scientific instruments.

His journey east pre-dated the opening of the Suez Canal, and so he crossed from Alexandria to the head of the Red Sea by the 'overland' route and thence via Aden and Bombay. His ship, the *Pottinger*, arrived in Singapore on 18 April 1854. His account of the countryside in what is now the city-state of the Republic of Singapore is of interest:

> The island of Singapore consists of a multitude of small hills, three or four hundred feet [90 to 120 m] high. The summits of many of which are still covered with virgin forest . . . much frequented by wood-cutters and sawyers, and [which] offered me an excellent collecting ground for insects. Here and there, too, were tiger pits, carefully covered over with sticks and leaves, and so well concealed that in several cases I had a narrow escape from falling into them . . . There are always a few tigers roaming about in Singapore, and they kill on average a Chinaman every day, principally those who work in the gambir[5] plantations . . . We heard a tiger roar once or twice in the evening: it was rather nervous work hunting for insects . . . when one of these savage animals might be lurking close by (*MA*, chap. II).[6]

The alarming statement that tigers ate 'a Chinaman every day' was completely erroneous (although humans were sometimes killed), but in the course of his peregrinations through Southeast Asia, there were other animals that sometimes posed a threat to Wallace's safety, or at least to his sense of security. One evening in Amboyna (now Ambon Island) he heard a strange noise in the thatched roof of his hut, but quickly fell asleep and thought little of it. The next afternoon, just before dinner, Wallace was lying down reading after a tiring day's work when, glancing upwards, he saw a large yellow-and-black mass of something overhead which he had not noticed before. He recalled:

Local worker extracting a python from Wallace's hut at Amboyna (Ambon), in an illustration from his *The Malay Archipelago* (1869).

> A python had climbed up one of the posts of the house, and had made his way under the thatch within a yard of my head, and taken up a comfortable position in the roof – and I had slept soundly all night directly under him (*MA*, I, chap. xx).

Eventually, a local plantation worker with a noose made of rattan in one hand and a long pole in the other, poked at the enormous snake, which then gradually began to uncoil itself. The man managed to slip the noose over its head and, getting it well over the body, pulled the animal down. There was a scuffle as the snake coiled itself round chairs and posts to resist its captor, but eventually the man caught hold of its tail and pulled it out of the house, dashed its head against a tree and killed it with a hatchet. It was found to be about 3.67 m (12 ft) in length. The skin is preserved at the premises of the Linnean Society of London; it was found to be a full-grown Moluccan python (*Morelia clastolepis*).

On another occasion, while trying to get to sleep on board ship, he put out his hand for his handkerchief and, as he put it, 'I quickly drew back on feeling something cool and very smooth which moved when I touched it.' When a light was brought, the creature was found to be 'nicely coiled up, with his head just raised to inquire who had disturbed him'. Wallace killed the reptile with a chopping knife, discovering that it had large poison fangs!

A letter written from Macassar on 1 December 1856 to Samuel Stevens (the agent who once again sold the specimens he collected and forwarded to England) provided an indication of a few of the difficulties under which he lived and worked, but also gives a hint of the friendly relations between the two men:

> After this you will probably not receive another letter from me for six or seven months, so I must give you a full one now. I am busy packing up my collections here, but have unfortunately been caught by the rains before I have finished, and I fear my insects will suffer. The last four or five days have been blowing, rainy weather, like our February, barring the cold. In a bamboo house, full of pores and cracks and crannies, through which the damp finds its way at pleasure, you may fancy it will not do to close up boxes of insects during such weather.
>
> The neighbourhood of Macassar has much disappointed me. After great trouble I discovered a place I thought promising, and after more trouble got the use of a native house there. I staid [*sic*] five weeks, and worked hard, though all the time ill (owing to bad water I think), and often . . . unable to do more than watch about the house for stray insects. Such a weakness and languor had seized me that often, on returning with some insects, I could hardly rise from my mattress.[7]

Wallace's modus operandi was to travel to a particular place and then use it as a base for a period of several days or weeks. Wherever possible he used a room of the house in which he was living for scientific work, but conditions were seldom easy. Here is an account of his stay in the southwest of Lombok, in August 1854:

One small room had to serve for eating, sleeping and working, for storehouse and dissecting room; in it were no shelves, cupboards, chair or tables; ants swarmed in every part of it, and dogs, cats and fowls entered it at pleasure. Besides this it was the parlour and reception room of my host . . . My principal piece of furniture was a box, which served me as a dining table, a seat while skinning birds and a receptacle of the birds when skinned and dried. To keep them free from ants we borrowed . . . an old bench, the four legs of which being placed in cocoa-nut shells filled with water kept us tolerably free from these pests. The box and the bench were however literally the only places where anything could be put away, and they were generally occupied by two insect boxes and about a hundred birds in the process of drying . . . When anything bulky or out of the common way was collected, the question 'where is it to be put?' was rather a difficult one to answer. All animal substances moreover require some time to dry thoroughly, emit a disagreeable odour while doing so, and are particularly attractive to ants, flies, dogs, cats and other vermin, calling for especial cautions and constant supervision, which under the circumstance above described were impossible (MA, chap. x).

At Wayapi, on the island of Bouru, in May 1861 he was working from a 'low hut with a very rotten roof through which the sky could be seen in several places'. Sometimes for weeks at a time he was confined to his lodging by the weather, or illness prevented him from venturing out on collecting trips.

Wallace's plan to finance his travels by sending collections of specimens back to the reliable Samuel Stevens in London for sale seems to have been reasonably successful: a typical consignment sent in August 1856 included 300 bird specimens, 150 butterflies in folded papers, 250 beetle specimens and 100 land and freshwater shells. He hoped to obtain £60 for this collection (perhaps the equivalent of some £7,000 in 2018).[8]

But the 'species question' seems to have never been far from his mind. On arriving in the Malay Archipelago, he decided 'to keep a complete set of certain groups from every island or distinct locality', in order to ascertain the 'geographical distribution of animals of the Archipelago, and to throw light on various other problems'. He regretted he had not adopted the same approach in South America (*Life*, 1, 385).

During the eight years he was in the East Indies, he undertook some seventy different expeditions – including a combined total of around 22,000 kilometres (*c.* 14,000 mi.) of travel. He visited every important island in what is now the Indonesian archipelago at least once, and some of them several times. His period of residence in the islands adjacent to New Guinea was particularly important, as he was one of the very first Europeans to live there for an extended period.

Wallace's collecting (his own collections plus specimens gathered by a small army of assistants, some of whom were only with him for a few weeks or months) resulted in him accumulating a total of 125,660 specimens, including over a thousand species then new to science. Insects were his special concern: he estimated that after three-and-a-half years in the archipelago, he had collected 8,540 species of insects. The book that came out of his journeyings, *The Malay Archipelago*, is the most celebrated of all natural history writings on the East Indies. Particularly significant were his accounts of his studies and capture of birds of paradise and orang-utans, as well as his work on some of the region's spectacular butterflies. He was impressed by their beauty: of particular species of swallowtail butterfly, he wrote that some had 'crimson or golden patches, which when viewed from a certain angle change to . . . opalescent hues, unsurpassed by the rarest gems'.

Wallace was, as has been mentioned, one of the first naturalists to make a systematic study of the behaviour of organisms, particularly birds. He wrote that what he 'valued almost as much as the birds themselves was the knowledge of their habits'. The great bird of paradise held 'dancing parties' or *sácaleli* in certain conspicuous trees in the forest, which

> [had] an immense head of spreading branches and . . . large but scattered leaves giving a clear space for the birds to play and exhibit their plumes. On one of these trees a dozen or twenty full-plumaged male birds assemble together, raise up their wings, stretch out their necks, and elevate their exquisite plumes, keeping them in continual vibration . . . They fly across from branch to branch in great excitement, so that the whole tree is filled with waving plumes in every variety of attitude and motion. The bird itself . . . is of a rich coffee brown colour. The head and neck is of a pure straw yellow above, and rich metallic green beneath. The long plumy tufts of golden orange feathers spring from the sides beneath each wing, and when the bird is in repose are partly concealed by them. At the time of its excitement, however, the wings are raised vertically over the back, the head is bent down and stretched out, and the long plumes are expanded till they form two magnificent golden fans striped with deep red at the base . . . The whole bird is overshadowed by them, the crouching body, yellow head, and emerald green throat forming but the foundation and setting to the glory which waves above (*MA*, chap. xxxi).

Wallace did not attempt to explain or interpret the behaviour of the birds of paradise; nevertheless, in the passage above, and others like it, he shows how behaviour, appearance and, to some extent, habitat are intertwined. Later authors have emphasized the role of communal *lek* or *arena* displays in increasing the spectacular

Aru islanders shooting the Great Bird of Paradise at a 'dancing party', the frontispiece to the second volume of Wallace's *Malay Archipelago* (1869).

nature, volume or 'reach' of the courtship performance. A group of males displaying on a conspicuous site is more likely to attract females than a single male alone. Such elaborate performances may also contribute to the synchronization of the sexual rhythms of the males and females. Lek systems in birds are sometimes associated with sexual dimorphism (the existence of marked differences between the sexes), which is itself, it is argued, partly the product of sexual selection – the females selecting those males in the arena that have the most spectacular plumage and attractive display.[9] Sometimes, without knowing or fully understanding their importance, Wallace was making observations that were of profound evolutionary significance.

Another instance of this is provided by his account of adaptation as regards the great shielded grasshopper of New Guinea, which had a 'thorax covered by a large triangular horny shield, two and a half inches long, with serrated edges . . . and a faint median line, so as to very closely resemble a leaf'. He continued,

> The glossy wing-coverts . . . are of a fine green colour and so beautifully veined as to imitate closely some of the shining tropical leaves . . . These insects are sluggish in their motions, depending for safety on their resemblance to foliage, their horny shield and wing coverts and their spiny legs (MA, chap. XXXIX).

Once again habitat, behaviour and appearance are shown to be tightly integrated.

Nevertheless, despite his perceptiveness, Wallace's descriptions of animal behaviour were sometimes extremely anthropomorphic – attributing human emotions to non-human creatures. A letter from central Sumatra – 'the very land of monkeys' – in December 1861 describes how they swarmed around the plantations and villages:

The great shielded grasshopper (*Siliquofera grandis*, formerly *Megalodon ensifer*), showing its remarkable camouflage, in an illustration from Wallace's *Malay Archipelago* (1869).

They are eternally racing about the tree-tops and gambolling in the most amusing manner . . . They throw themselves recklessly through the air, apparently sure, with one of their four hands, to catch hold of something. I estimated one jump by a long-tailed white monkey at 30 feet [9 m] horizontal & 60 feet [18 m] vertical from a high tree onto a lower one; he fell through, however, so great was his impetus, on to a still lower branch, and then without a moment's stop, scampered away . . . evidently quite pleased with his pluck. When I startle a band, and one leader takes a leap like this, it is amusing to watch the others, some afraid and hesitating on the brink till at last they pluck up courage, take a run at it, and often roll over in the air with their desperate efforts (*Life*, I, 381).

It is perhaps unsurprising that he attributed human emotions strongly to the orang-utan – or *mias*, as the local folk called it. In May 1855 he was hunting orang-utans in Borneo. He described a male on which he fired as being 'in a great rage', and another was 'howling and hooting with rage' (*MA*, chap. IV). An orphaned youngster, when presented with a finger to suck, but from which it could not extract milk, 'after persevering for a long time would ... give up in distrust, and set up a scream very like that of a [human] baby in similar circumstances. When handled or nursed it was very quiet and contented.' When washed, this orang-utan would 'wince' and 'make wry faces' as cold water rushed over it. The creature seemed 'pleased' when put to hang from a small ladder, was 'fond' of hair and Wallace's beard and 'would turn up its eyes in supreme satisfaction when it had a mouthful particularly to its taste.' This youngster became 'excellent friends' with a young hare-lip monkey with which it was enclosed and climbed over the monkey irrespective of its 'feelings'. The evolutionary affinity of the orang-utan and the other apes with humans is hinted at in the following sentence:

> With what interest must every naturalist look forward to the time when the caves and tertiary deposits of the tropics may be thoroughly examined, and the past history and earliest appearance of the great man-like apes be at length made known (*MA*, chap. IV).[10]

Wallace here is imputing a series of human reactions and emotions to the primates he encountered. Although he seems to have perceived an affinity between humans and monkeys and apes, he did not allow it to affect the rather brutal manner in which he slaughtered – by shooting – a total of eighteen orang-utans to obtain specimens of skins and skeletons. These included the mother of the orphaned baby mentioned above. The nineteenth was shot but escaped. In later life, however, he was quite conservation-minded. (It will later be shown that while Wallace was happy applying the broad principles of evolution to the human form, he was less happy with applying them to the human mind and moral character.)

'Orang-utan attacked by Dyaks', the frontispiece to the first volume of Wallace's *Malay Archipelago* (1869).

Wallace also compiled detailed accounts of indigenous people, and in an Appendix to *The Malay Archipelago*, he gives a comparative vocabulary of 'One hundred and seventeen words in thirty-three languages of the Malay Archipelago'. As well as describing house-types, customs and social structures, he also, like other travellers of the Victorian period, sometimes dwells upon the sensational, the titillating and the bizarre:

> Serious infidelity is punished . . . cruelly, the woman and her paramour being tied back to back and thrown into the sea, where some large crocodiles are always on the watch to devour the bodies. One such execution took place while I was at Ampanam, but I took a long walk into the country to be out of the way until it was all over, thus missing the opportunity of having a horrible narrative to enliven my somewhat tedious story (*MA*, chap. XI).

One day while on the island of Lombok, he was informed that there was an 'Amok' in the village – a man was 'running amok'. The gates were immediately closed, but after hearing nothing for some time, Wallace went out to investigate – it had been a false alarm. A slave had run away, declaring he would 'amok' because his master wanted to sell him.

> A short time before, a man had been killed at a gaming-table because, having lost half-a-dollar more than he possessed, he was going to 'amok'. Another had killed or wounded seventeen people before he could be destroyed. In their wars, a whole regiment of these people will sometimes agree to 'amok', and then rush on with such energetic desperation as to be very formidable to men not so excited as themselves (*MA*, chap. XI).

On one of his journeys through Lombok's countryside, Wallace's attention was drawn to a couple of human skeletons, enclosed within small bamboo fences, with the 'clothes, pillow, mat and betel box of the unfortunate individual – who had been either murdered or executed' (MA, chap. X).

In describing such incidents, there was often no attempt to explain or interpret. The observations stand alone . . . the reader is left wondering. While Wallace's observations on the physical features of animals or plants are 'connected' – as he tries to discern broad patterns, explain and interpret (for example, attempting to show relationships among the morphologies, habitats and behaviours of organisms) – his observations on humanity tend to be anecdotal, or one-off remarks. He enjoys a good tale and suspects his readers will too, occasionally not appearing to care, as he himself once put it, 'whether it is altogether true or not'. He had something of the Victorian age's obsession with things strange, bizarre and exotic.

As in South America, Wallace had to contend with assistants who abandoned him at critical times. Travel and the physical business of collecting were sometimes fiendishly difficult: in the thorny scrub of southwest Lombok, 'everything grew zigzag and jagged and in an inextricable tangle' so that it was impossible to get through the bush 'with gun or net or even spectacles'. He was also often unwell, sometimes weak through lack of food – partly because he had to wait for long periods until money from the sale of his specimens came through.

On the Indonesian island of Ternate he experienced an earth-quake, which he described vividly: 'I had just awoke at . . . 5 a.m., when suddenly the thatch began to rustle and shake as if an army of cats were galloping over it, and immediately afterwards my bed shook too' (MA, chap. XXI). The earthquake was not serious but he described the incident as 'exciting', as the place had frequently in the past, most recently in February 1840, been completely destroyed by earthquakes.

A letter that Wallace sent home in May 1855 from up-country in Borneo summarizes some of the other difficulties and worries with which he had to contend: he had 'a continual struggle to get enough to eat', as all the chickens raised and vegetables grown by the local Dyak people were sold out of the area. Head-hunting had only been abandoned a few years previously, and the old men related with pride how many 'heads' they had taken in their youth; they had the idea that if they were allowed to take a few heads, as of old, they would have better crops! Such knowledge would on occasion make the visitor anxious (*MA*, chap. x).

On the other hand, the following extract (taken from his account of the island of Amboyna, or Ambon Island, where he spent December 1857), giving an idea of the way in which he lived and worked, conveys something of the contentment he must have felt when things were going well:

My abode was merely a little thatched hut, consisting of an open verandah in front and a small dark sleeping room behind. It was raised about five feet [1.5 m] from the ground, and was reached by rude steps to the centre of the verandah. The walls and floor were of bamboo, and it contained a table, two bamboo chairs, and a couch. Here I soon made myself comfortable, and set to work hunting for insects among the more recently felled timber, which swarmed with fine Curculionidae, Longicorns, and Buprestidae most of them remarkable for their elegant forms or brilliant colours, and almost all entirely new to me. Only the entomologist can appreciate the delight with which I hunted about for hours in the hot sunshine, among the branches and twigs and bark of the fallen trees, every few minutes securing insects which were at that time almost all rare or new to European collections . . . Of an evening I generally sat reading in the verandah, ready to capture any insects that were attracted to the light (*MA*, chap. xx).

Wallace was eight long years in Southeast Asia, and he was active in collecting and observing throughout, often in the most remote locations and under difficult, sometimes quite dangerous, conditions. Here he is describing his adventures towards the conclusion of his sojourn, at the end of 1862, a matter of weeks before he returned to England, in a letter to an old schoolfriend:

> I am here in one of the places unknown to the Royal Geog. Soc. situated in the very centre of E. Sumatra, 100 miles from the sea all round. It is the height of the wet season, & pours down strong & steady, generally all night & half the day. Bad times for me, but I walk out regularly for 3 or 4 hours every day, picking up what I can, & generally getting some little new or rare or beautiful thing to reward me. This is the land of the two horned Rhinoceros, the Elephant, the tiger and the tapir . . . once [I heard] a rhinoceros bark not far off.[11]

Perhaps to allay his old friend's fears, he added the note that 'beyond their track & their dung' he was often 'not aware of their [the large mammals] existence'.

Wallace was a superb observer: his letters (such as the above) and other writings are full of fine detail. He was prepared to utilize his observations to make generalizations, and to build theories. Wallace later became especially known for his proposal of a regional boundary which was then termed 'Wallace's Line'. This extended between the islands of Bali and Lombok, and between Borneo and Sulawesi, marking the limits of eastern extent of many Asian forms and, conversely, the limits of the western extent of many Australasian forms:

> The great contrast between the two divisions of the Archipelago is nowhere so abruptly exhibited as on passing from the island of Bali to that of Lombok where the two regions are in close proximity. In Bali we have barbets, fruit-thrushes and

Wallace soon after returning from his travels, 1862.

woodpeckers; on passing to Lombok these are seen no more, but we have an abundance of cockatoos, honeysuckers and brush-turkeys, which are equally unknown in Bali or any island further west. The strait here is fifteen miles wide, so that we may pass in two hours from one great division of the world to another (*MA*, chap. I).

The concept of Wallace's Line has profoundly affected the development of biogeography and indeed the whole modern idea of plate tectonics, which assumes that the Australian crustal plate converged on that of Asia over the last few tens of millions of years. As the islands of what is now Indonesia were thrown up by this convergence, there was a flow of life-forms between land surfaces on the two plates. This junction is now perhaps more accurately thought of as a *zone* rather than a *line*. The Balinese fauna contains more 'Australian' taxa than the above quotation suggests. A lorikeet (*Trichoglossus haematodus*) occurred until recently; so too did the scrubfowl,[12] and a species of honeyeater also crosses the 'line'.

The notion of the transmutability of species remained at the back of his mind and while in Sarawak, Borneo, in February 1855, he penned a paper, 'On the Law Which Has Regulated the Introduction of New Species', which was accepted by the *Annals and Magazine of Natural History* and published in September 1855 (xvi, 2nd Series, pp. 184–96). Wallace's 'law' stated that 'Every species has come into existence coincident in space and time with a pre-existing closely allied species.'

The article was theoretical, but argued from the point of view of the natural affinities between organisms, the fossil record and analysis of the geographical distributions of plants and animals – all drawn from utilizing his experience of both South America and the Malay Archipelago. Wallace states that throughout the 'immense, but unknown' period of geological time, enormous 'successive changes' had taken place, and that during this whole series of changes the 'organic life of the earth has undergone a corresponding alteration' and 'the present condition of the natural world is clearly derived by a natural process of gradual extinction and creation of species from that of the latest geological periods.'

He went on to state that any species would have had 'for its immediate antitype, a closely allied species that existed at the time of its origin'. He speculated that a number of species might be placed in 'direct succession, in a straight line'. However, sometimes a forked or many-branched line might exist – he used the metaphor of the branching tree. Wallace noted that islands and areas separated from neighbouring districts by high mountains had distinctive faunas. And particularly significant is the following:

> The shallow sea between the Peninsula of Malacca, Java and Sumatra and Borneo was probably a continent or large island at an early epoch, and may have become submerged as the volcanic ranges of Java and Sumatra were elevated. The organic results we see in the very considerable number of species of animals common to some or all of these countries, while at the same time a number of closely allied representative species exist peculiar to each, showing that a considerable period has elapsed since their separation. The facts of geographical distribution and of geology may thus mutually explain each other . . .

In this paper, too, Wallace puzzles over the meaning of the existence of rudimentary organs, such as 'the minute limbs hidden beneath the skin of . . . snake-like lizards' and the 'jointed finger bones in the paddle of the . . . whale'. He continues:

> To every thoughtful naturalist the question must arise, What are these [organs] for? . . . Do they not teach us something of the system of Nature? If each species had been created independently, and without any necessary relations with pre-existing species, what do these rudiments, these apparent

imperfections mean? There must be a cause for them; they must be the necessary results of some great natural law. Now, if, as it has been endeavoured to be shown, the great law which has regulated the peopling of the earth with animal and vegetable life is, that every change shall be gradual; that no new creature shall be formed widely differing from anything before existing; that in this, as in everything else in Nature, there shall be graduation and harmony, – these rudimentary organs are necessary, and are an essential part of the system of Nature.

The paper implies, but does not actually state, that there has been a progression of life-forms on the planet throughout geological time. The paper received an unspectacular reception in Britain. It did, however, provide a framework for Wallace's thoughts as he continued his travels, collecting and observing the variety of living things in Southeast Asia.

And then, in a hut on a remote island, while once again racked by fever, exactly three years after this earlier insight, it all came together.[13]

4

The Natural Selection Insight
and Its Aftermath

In fact, although his actual insight seemed quite sudden, Wallace had been moving towards it for some months. He was probably thinking a great deal about the 'species question' in the months following the writing and publication in 1855 of what has become known as 'the Sarawak paper' (see Chapter Three). From early January to March 1857 he was based at Dobbo (now usually written 'Dobo') in the northern Aru Islands – a group of low, forested islands that are now part of Indonesia but lie quite close to the island of New Guinea.[1] He describes how 'he had the good fortune to capture one of the most magnificent insects the world contains the great bird-winged butterfly *Ornithoptera poseidon*.' He continued:

> I trembled with excitement as I saw it coming majestically towards me, and could hardly believe I had really succeeded in my stroke till I had taken it out of the net and was gazing, lost in admiration, at the velvet black and brilliant green of its wings, seven inches [18 cm] across, its golden body, and crimson breast . . . I had seen similar insects in cabinets at home, but it is quite another thing to capture such one's self . . . and to gaze upon its fresh and living beauty, a bright gem shining out amid the silent gloom of a dark and tangled forest (*MA*, chap. xxx).

So wrote Wallace some years later, in *The Malay Archipelago*, first published in 1869. At the time, he seems to have been unsure of the

Eighteenth-century illustrations of *Papilio priamus* (now *Ornithopertera [priamus] poseidon*), 'One of the most magnificent insects the world contains', from Pieter Crarer, *De Uitlandsche Kapellen* (1775–82).

exact identification of the creature. In a short article that must have been written not long after the incident described above – which occurred in mid-January 1857 – he describes the beautiful insect as 'very closely allied to *Ornithoptera poseidon*, of which it may be a variety'. Yet the title of the piece is 'On the Habits and Transformation of a Species of *Ornithoptera* Allied to *O. priamus* Inhabiting the Aru Islands, near New Guinea'. It rather looks as though he was somewhat uncertain of the exact taxonomic status of this beautiful creature. And well he might be: the insect is now usually known by the scientific name *Ornithoptera priamus* (a name originally given a century earlier by the Swedish naturalist Linnaeus), but some 99 sub-species or varieties have been described. Moreover, there is also considerable variation *within* a sub-species. One source of variation is in the number of spots on the butterfly's hindwing.

A further complication is that the insect is strongly dimorphic: the female is of a completely different appearance to the male – a drab brown. Forms are known from throughout Southeast Asia, New Guinea and northern Australia. The trinomial (three-fold name) *Ornithoptera priamus poseidon* is often used for the variety or sub-species of birdwing that is found in the Torres Strait Islands, New Guinea and some adjacent islands.

It may well have been the uncertainty in his mind about the status of the birdwing specimens he had collected on Aru, and an appreciation of this species' variability (although he could not possibly have known its true extent) that encouraged him to write another short paper at about the same time as, or only a few weeks later than, the *Ornithoptera* article mentioned above – it was published in London early in 1858 – with the intriguing title 'Note on the Theory of Permanent and Geographical Varieties'. The essay was very short and entirely theoretical (he gave no detailed examples), but one is tempted to assume that he had the striking birdwing butterflies in his mind.[2]

An illustration of Dobbo in New Guinea, where Wallace had a theoretical breakthrough, from his *Malay Archipelago* (1869).

Scientific opinion at the time allowed *some* mutability within species: such differences accounted for the varieties, such as geographical varieties, frequently found in nature. But differences between what are recognized as species might be exceedingly minute, so that, he wrote, 'a species differs from a variety in degree only, not in nature, and no two persons will agree as to the amount of difference to constitute the one, or the amount of resemblance which must exist to form the other.' He continued, asking,

> why should a special act of creation be required to call into existence an organism differing only in degree from one which has been produced by existing laws? If an amount of permanent difference, represented by any number up to ten, may be produced by the ordinary course of nature, it is surely most illogical and very hard to believe, that an amount of difference represented by 11 required a special act of creation to call it into existence.

Wallace thus appreciated that there were, in fact, gradations between species. He was very close indeed to a revolutionary insight. In his 1855 Sarawak paper he had propounded the law: 'Every species has come into existence coincident in space and time with a pre-existing closely allied species.' In this same paper, he had also stressed that the 'organic life of the earth has undergone . . . alteration' through much of geological time, and that 'the present condition of the natural world is clearly derived by a natural process of gradual extinction and creation of species from that of the latest geological periods.'

By late 1857, therefore, Wallace had accepted, in his own mind the following:

- That there had been immense changes in organic life on Earth, and that new species had appeared and others had become extinct throughout geological time.

- That species sometimes graded one into another through a series of varieties.
- That species had 'come into existence coincident in space and time with pre-existing closely allied species'.
- That, therefore, it seemed possible that one *species* might change into another, and that occasionally a bifurcating or branching genealogy could be envisaged.

He had gone into print, in well-known scientific journals, expounding these points, although not all at the same time. He had already shown, years before, through his correspondence with Bates about his appreciative reading of Chambers's book *Vestiges of the Natural History of Creation* (1844), that he was amenable to the idea of some form of evolutionary progression. And he had, some years previously in his *Narrative of Travels on the Amazon and Rio Negro*, used the phrases 'struggle for existence' and 'battle for life'.

In February 1858, while Wallace was suffering from an attack of what is very likely to have been malaria, in a remote village on the East Indian island of Ternate (Halmahera, the large adjacent island, has also been suggested), he received a spectacular insight – the notion that evolutionary change (the idea that he, and others, had been flirting with for some years) might be powered by natural selection.

During one of the bouts of malaria that he suffered, so he wrote later, he recalled Malthus's essay on population, with its idea that 'checks' kept human populations more or less stable. Such checks might act on all organisms. Many species of animals, he realized, produce far more young than could possibly survive to adulthood. He put this idea together with his understanding of variations that occurred continually, along with an appreciation of changes in the climate and other aspects of the environment that had continued throughout geological time – Wallace was profoundly influenced by Charles Lyell's *Principles of Geology* (1st edn, 3 vols, 1830–32).

Charles Lyell, *c*. 1865, wood engraving.

When he felt a little better, he wrote an essay setting out his ideas: 'On the Tendency of Varieties to Depart Indefinitely from the Original Type'. In this, he instanced the possibility that a pair of birds produced two young a year, for four years. Then, he argued, without checks, 'A simple calculation will show that in fifteen years each pair would have increased to nearly ten millions!', yet the numbers of many species remained approximately constant. There would thus be a struggle for existence in which 'the weakest and least perfectly organised must always succumb'. (He had used this phrase and 'battle for life' some years earlier.) It would be the 'superior' creatures that survived, and the 'inferior' variations that would perish. Gradually a 'superior' variety would displace the original parent species. Thus 'certain varieties have a tendency to maintain their existence longer than the original species, and this tendency must make itself felt.' He concluded,

We believe we have now shown that there is a tendency in nature to the continued progression of certain classes of varieties further and further from the original type – a progression to which there appears no reason to assign any definite limits . . . This progression, by minute steps, in various directions, but always checked and balanced by the necessary conditions, subject to which alone existence can be preserved, may, it is believed, be followed out so as to agree with all the phenomena presented by organized beings, their extinction and succession in past ages, and all the extraordinary modifications of form, instinct, and habits which they exhibit.

He sent the paper, together with a covering letter, to Charles Darwin, who he knew from previous correspondence was interested in the 'species question'. He asked Darwin to pass the essay on to Charles Lyell if he thought it was sufficiently interesting. Wallace had never corresponded with Lyell, although he was one of the most respected scientists of the day, and in an earlier letter to Wallace, Darwin had stated that Lyell had found the former's 1855 paper of interest. Some portion of this earlier correspondence between Darwin and Wallace is, at this point, worth reviewing briefly (although part has been lost).

Around December 1855, Darwin had written to Wallace, along with some thirty other naturalists in different parts of the world, seeking skins of 'Any domestic breed of Poultry, pigeons, rabbits, cats & even dogs if not too large' for his researches on variation. (Darwin was seeking material for his book *The Variation of Animals and Plants under Domestication*, which eventually appeared in January 1868; he also makes considerable reference to variation under domestic conditions in his *Origin of Species*.) Darwin had read the Sarawak paper in the *Annals and Magazine of Natural History*, approved of it, and told Wallace so. He wrote to Wallace on 1 May 1857, in reply to a letter dated October 1856, as follows:

By your letter & even still more by your paper in the Annals . . .
I can plainly see that we have thought much alike & to a certain
extent have come to similar conclusions. In regard to the paper
in Annals, I agree to the truth of every word.
. . .
  This summer will make the 20th year (!) since I opened my
first note-book, on the question how & in what way do species
& varieties differ from each other. – I am now preparing my work
for publication, but I find the subject so very large, that though
I have written many chapters, I do not suppose I shall go to press
for two years.[3]

Clearly Darwin was assuring Wallace of the importance of the
subjects of variation and the nature of species, and of his interest
in them, but can we not also detect a trace of posturing: 'Beware,
this is my territory: I got here first'? Wallace, by sending his 1858
paper to Darwin is appreciating the first part of this, but
presumably did not pick up on the second.

In the 1858 paper, Wallace used the term 'struggle for existence'
and, further, he argued by analogy from domestic animals to those
found in nature: just as humans had selected for particular
characteristics in farm animals, so the natural environment had
imposed selection processes on those in the wild. Darwin argued
in an exactly analogous manner.

Unknown to Wallace, Darwin had hit upon the idea of natural
selection many years earlier. Some of his arguments were identical.
Darwin was therefore extremely concerned when he received
Wallace's letter and the paper (probably on 18 June 1858) and at
once consulted two of his scientific friends – geologist Lyell and
botanist Joseph Hooker – as to what he should do. Darwin was,
of course, worried that despite over twenty years of work, he might
lose scientific priority, although two of his children were gravely
ill, and it seems likely that his mind was distracted.

Lyell and Hooker to some extent took the matter out of Darwin's hands and decided to present Wallace's essay (without his full knowledge, which would have been impossible to obtain at short notice), along with two hitherto unpublished extracts from Darwin's writings on the subject, at a meeting of the Linnean Society of London on 1 July 1858. Although the reading of the joint presentation was the first item of business at the meeting, there were other papers before the thirty or so members present that evening, and there does not seem to have been very much discussion. The combined offering was published in the Society's journal a few weeks later.[4] Darwin was not present at the meeting: he had other matters of concern to him. He had to attend the funeral of his youngest son (Charles Waring) at home in Kent while one of his daughters (Henrietta) was also very ill – as was his niece, who died a fortnight later. Darwin's son George was being kept in isolation with measles at his school.

A photograph of Charles Darwin in middle life, taken c. 1854.

Joseph Hooker, *c.* 1860s, wood engraving.

The combined Darwin-Wallace offering was titled, 'On the Tendency of Species to Form Varieties, and on the Perpetuation of Varieties and Species by Natural Means of Selection'. Darwin's contributions were placed above Wallace's essay, emphasizing his priority in date. Wallace later commented that the paper was published without his having any chance of polishing it, and (as he put it later to the German anthropologist A. B. Meyer in 1869), 'of course without any correction of proofs'. This despite Lyell and Hooker's statement given at the head of the joint submission that 'both authors . . . [have] unreservedly placed their papers in our hands.'[5]

There is evidence that Darwin felt somewhat guilty about all this. And indeed the incident has been referred to by some as a 'moral lapse', even if forgivable in the face of the enormous strain that he was under, and the fact that Wallace was a world away. Nevertheless Wallace, whatever his inner feelings, seems outwardly to have taken the matter in good spirit, and the two remained friends and colleagues. In fact, Wallace said later that he had been 'highly gratified' by what had been done with his essay and continued a sporadic correspondence with both Darwin and Hooker. Darwin wrote to Wallace in late January 1859,

> I was extremely much pleased at receiving three days ago your letter to me and that to Dr Hooker. Permit me to say how heartily I admire the spirit in which they are written. Though I had absolutely nothing whatever to do in leading Lyell & Hooker to what they thought a fair course of action, yet I naturally could not but feel anxious to hear what your impression would be . . . Everyone I have seen has thought your paper very well written & interesting.[6]

Some have asserted that Wallace felt he had been ill-treated by Darwin (and by Hooker and Lyell), but there is not the slightest evidence of this. Wallace dedicated his book *The Malay Archipelago* (1869) to Charles Darwin 'not only as a token of personal esteem and friendship, but also to express my deep admiration for his genius and his works'. He also published a book on evolution entitled *Darwinism* in 1889. Nor does the Wallace family seem to have harboured any grudge. His grandson John stated in 1990, 'I can't understand what all the fuss is about. Grandfather was satisfied with the arrangement, none of us desire to call it "Wallace's theory of natural selection" but many of the Darwin people seem defensive about it.'[7]

However, the incident prompted Darwin almost immediately to abandon writing the 'Big Book'[8] on evolution on which he was working (and which he referred to in his May 1857 letter to Wallace), and instead set about producing a more concise 'abstract' of what he had written up until that point. This 'abstract' was published some fifteen months after the appearance of the Linnean Society paper, in November 1859, as Charles Darwin's most famous book: *On the Origin of Species*.

Wallace was a little over thirty when he arrived at the theory of evolution through natural selection: he had before him another sixty years of his scientific career. During this time he used, and developed, the evolutionary idea in a great variety of ways. Only a few of these can be detailed here, but some of the work of his mature years is outlined in the chapter that follows and includes interesting and spectacular uses of the theory employed in explaining the colouration of organisms.

5

The Maturing Scientist

Wallace departed the East Indies on 8 February 1862, with his notes and his specimens; he had also sent many thousands of specimens back to Britain over the preceding eight years. The specimens he took with him included two living birds of paradise destined for London Zoo: they were fed partly on cockroaches which 'abound on every ship in the tropics!' On reaching England on 31 March (his notebook records 1 April), he hoped that his collecting activities over the preceding years would earn him a substantial sum. He planned to retire to the quiet life as a country gentleman, and indeed the sale of specimens did support him for a while.

Regarding specimens, as well as having thousands for sale, Wallace – a near-obsessive collector from his teenage years onwards – had a vast personal collection and a powerful desire to *own* them. Shortly after making Bates's acquaintance – and thus that of beetle collecting – Wallace wrote to him on 13 October 1845:

> I shall be much obliged to you for any of the following of which you can send me good specimens.
> *Chlaenius vestitus*
> *Ophonus azureus*
> *Chrysomela hyperici*
> *Brachinus crepitans . . .*[1]

Nearly ten years later (9 May 1854) he seemed greatly preoccupied by the numbers of various beetle taxa he had collected in Singapore:

> I have 6 species of Cicindelas [tiger beetles], all small;
> 13 Carabidae [ground beetles], mostly minute, but very
> beautiful; 10–12 Cleridae [chequered beetles]; about
> 30 very small Curculionidae [weevils]; and *mirabile dictu*!
> 50 species of Longicornes [long-horned beetles], and it is
> only 10 days since I took the first. Imagine my delight at
> taking 8 to 10 a day of this beautiful group . . .[2]

In about two months in Singapore, he later claimed, 'I obtained no less than 700 specimens of beetles . . . among them were 130 distinct species.' And at the Simunjon coalmines in Borneo,

> When I arrived at the mines, on 14 March [1855] I had collected,
> in the four preceding months, 320 different kinds of beetles. In
> less than a fortnight I had doubled this number, an average of

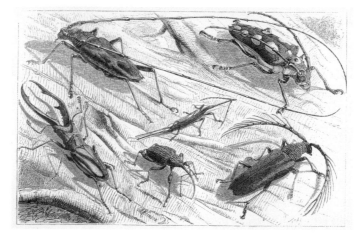

'Remarkable Beetles found at Simunjon, Borneo', an illustration from Wallace's *Malay Archipelago* (1869).

24 new species every day. One day I collected 76 different kinds, of which 34 were new to me . . . I sometimes obtained fifty or sixty different kinds in a day (*MA*, chap. IV).

Extracts such as these reveal not only a strong commitment to collecting, for its own sake, but an obsession with the *numbers* collected. Thus the Preface to *The Malay Archipelago* of 1869 includes the following enumeration:

I find that my Eastern collections amounted to:
310 specimens of Mammalia

100	–	Reptiles
8,050	–	Birds
7,500	–	Shells
13,100	–	Lepidoptera
83,200	–	Coleoptera
13,400	–	other Insects
125,660		specimens of natural history

For the three years after he returned to England, he immersed himself in the sorting, classification and study of these 'Eastern Collections', publishing a series of scientific papers suggesting systematic revisions of the classification of several biological groups (particularly of insects and birds) and several other monographs. We have already noted that from his very early years Wallace searched for order, for pattern. It was almost another obsession, and is well illustrated by the titles of some of his papers. Of those written in 1862 and 1863 several are on the taxonomy or classification of organisms: 'Descriptions of Three New Species of *Pitta* from the Moluccas'; 'Notes on the Genus *Iphias*'. Several others are, in fact, mainly *lists* of species found in particular localities. He was always searching for order and pattern.

In these first three years or so after his return, he presented papers at some sixteen scientific meetings, such as at the British Association for the Advancement of Science and the Royal Geographical Society, as well as at the Entomological, Zoological, Linnean and Anthropological Societies. This was besides a large number of shorter notes and 'letters to the editor' published in well-known scientific journals. He became assimilated into the brotherhood of British scientists and effectively established the sub-discipline of biogeography – for example, reading a paper 'On the Geographical Distribution of Animal Life' at the British Association for the Advancement of Science meeting at Newcastle-upon-Tyne, on 1 September 1863.

This 'Geographical Distribution' paper attempted to show the close connection between the distribution of organisms and their geographical context. So it is perhaps not surprising that just a few weeks before delivering it, he had read 'On the Physical Geography of the Malay Archipelago' to the Royal Geographical Society (8 June 1863). This latter paper was particularly well received, as was commented immediately after it had been delivered:

THE PRESIDENT [of the Royal Geographical Society] remarked that as a geologist, he must say, in all the years he had been connected with the Society, he had never heard a paper read of a more luminous character, and which so bound together in the most perfect form all the branches of the science of natural history, more particularly as it developed the truths of geography upon what he considered to be its soundest basis, that of geological observation and analogy (*Journal of RGS*, 33, p. 210).

Wallace was a great integrator, and his genius was beginning to be recognized.

Nevertheless, in certain respects, the period from 1862 to the end of 1865 was a rather difficult time for Wallace. He was most eager to marry and to settle down. In a note to an old schoolfriend, George Silk, written just before Wallace left Singapore for his return to England, he had set out his aspirations in this direction in some detail:

On the question of marriage, we probably differ much. I believe a good wife to be the greatest blessing a man can enjoy & the only road to happiness but the qualifications I should look for are probably not such as would satisfy you. My opinions have changed much on this point. I now look at intellectual companionship as quite a secondary matter, & should my good stars ever send me an affectionate good tempered & domestic wife, I should care not one iota for accomplishments or even education.[3]

He had clearly been thinking about the matter for some time, and indeed, not very long after his return to England from Asia, he became engaged to someone identified cryptically in his autobiography as a Miss L. She was Marion Leslie, whose father regularly played chess with Wallace. The engagement was broken off after a year. It seems, as one biographer put it, that 'Wallace's social skills . . . appeared to be in their infancy.' We have already noted that he seems to have had difficulty with social relationships throughout much of his life. It is perhaps for this reason that, apart from the few months of school-teaching in Leicester, and possibly the earlier time with the clockmaker in Bedfordshire, he was never able to gain proper salaried employment. At one stage in the 1860s, he applied for the position of Assistant Secretary of the Royal Geographical Society – a post for which he might have assumed he was well qualified. It went to H. W. Bates – his companion on the expedition to South America. Wallace argued that he needed a job that would allow him time to work on his collections; but this may have been an excuse, at least to himself.

In fact, Wallace would marry Annie, the twenty-year-old daughter of botanist and keen gardener Walter Mitten, in 1866 (Wallace's own account stated that she was only eighteen – as noted, he was sometimes imprecise about dates). Life for Wallace was never without its trials, and one of their three children died a few years later.

On returning from the East Indies Wallace lived with his sister and her husband in London, and indeed for the next two decades he lived a somewhat unsettled life, staying with relatives or sometimes living in rented accommodation. Nevertheless, he was amazingly productive. In 1863, the year after his return, he produced some thirteen publications; in 1864, twenty; in each of 1865 and 1866 there were nine; in 1867 the total was eighteen, one of which was a paper entitled 'Ice Marks in North Wales', written on the basis of fieldwork done on his and Annie's honeymoon! And so it continued – in some years he published around 25 articles, many of them in distinguished journals, on an enormous variety of subjects.

One of his self-imposed tasks, of course, was to drive home the message of evolution through natural selection, and some of his publications from this period attempt to do exactly that. One of his best papers in this regard is 'On the Phenomena of Variation and Geographical Distribution as Illustrated by the Papilionidæ of the Malayan Region'. This was presented to the Linnean Society of London in March 1864 and published in the *Transactions* of that organization the following year.[4] Here he examined many species of swallowtail butterfly, considering their appearance, habitat, distribution and behaviour and showing how these are interrelated. With the aid of a number of superb colour plates, he showed how variation within and between species, assisted by the pressures of natural selection, goes some way to explain the great range of forms this group presents. (The phenomena of mimicry, cryptic colouration and warning colouration, discussed below, are all well illustrated by this group.) He dealt with both the larvae and the adult forms of the butterflies. An example of his arguments and concern for detail is given in the following brief passage from what was a long paper.

> The most characteristic feature of the Papilionidæ, however, and that on which I think insufficient stress has been laid, is undoubtedly the peculiar structure of the larvæ. These all

Papilo coön (now *Losario coon*), a swallowtail butterfly illustrated in Wallace's *Malay Archipelago* (1869).

possess an extraordinary organ situated on the neck, the well-known Y-shaped tentacle, which is entirely concealed in a state of repose, but which is capable of being suddenly thrown out by the insect when alarmed. When we consider this singular apparatus, which in some species is nearly half an inch long [1 cm], the arrangement of muscles for its protrusion and retraction, its perfect concealment during repose, its blood-red colour, and the suddenness with which it can be thrown out, we must, I think, be led to the conclusion that it serves as a protection to the larva by startling and frightening away some enemy when about to seize it, and is thus one of the causes which has led to the wide extension and maintained the permanence of this now dominant group. Those who believe that such peculiar structures can only have arisen by very minute successive variations, each one advantageous to its possessor, must see, in the possession of such an organ by one group, and its complete absence in every other, a proof of a very ancient origin and of very long-continued modification.

As mentioned above, Wallace was an excellent integrator. In his 1863 Royal Geographical Society paper 'On the Physical Geography of the Malay Archipelago', he gives a superb summary of what was known of the physical features, geology (especially the volcanoes), climate and distribution of plants and animals of the East Indies. He stated,

> It was first pointed out by Mr. George Windsor Earl, in a paper read before this Society [the RGS] eighteen years ago, that a shallow sea connected the great islands of Sumatra, Borneo, and Java, to the Asiatic continent, with which they generally agreed in their natural productions; while a similar shallow sea connected New Guinea and some of the adjacent islands to Australia. Owing, however, to that gentleman's imperfect knowledge of the natural history of the various islands, he did not fully appreciate the important results of this observation, and in fact in the same paper argued in favour of the former connection of Asia and Australia – a connection to which the whole bearing of the facts in physical geography and natural history is plainly opposed.[5]

He argued from basic principles. For example, there was a general principle, Wallace stated, 'of almost universal application',

> that when we find an island whose animals and plants exactly agree with those of an adjacent land, we look for evidence of its recent separation from that land. On the other hand, any remarkable diversity of natural productions forces on us the conclusion that the watery barrier which now exists has existed for a very long geological period. And when the diversity is almost total, not only in species but in larger group such as genera, families and orders, we conclude that these countries could never have been connected since our continents and oceans had assumed their present general outlines.[6]

Wallace drew attention to the fact that the 'great islands' of Java, Sumatra and Borneo have plants and animals that closely resemble those of adjoining parts of the continent of Asia. On these islands we see apes and monkeys: in the eastern islands of the archipelago, there are few – Wallace mentioned just one species in Celebes. The contrast between the fauna of Bali and that of the nearby island of Lombok, just 24 kilometres (15 mi.) to its east, is particularly strong, as has already been noted. So too have Wallace's observations on the differences between the birds of Bali and those of the islands to the east (see Chapter Three).

The division occurred in the plant kingdom also. In Timor, the commonest trees, he reported, 'are Eucalypti of several species, so characteristic of Australia', and other Australian plants are found in lesser abundance. The islands to the west had plant species that were more strongly Asian in their affinities.

With the paper, he published a map inscribed with a clear line between Bali and Lombok, between Celebes and Borneo, and between the Philippine island of Mindanao and the group of small

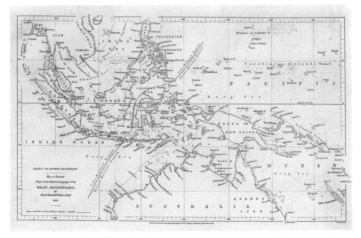

Map showing Wallace's line, from his 1863 paper on 'The Physical Geography of the Malay Archipelago'.

islands north of Celebes. West of what has become known as 'Wallace's Line' was the Indo-Malayan Region; to the east lay the Austro-Malayan Region.

Although the precise route of Wallace's Line has been a subject of argument among scientists in the years since it was suggested, the essential concept has been one of the pillars of biogeography. But the boundary is not as clear as the 1863 paper suggested. Cockatoos, and a single species of honeyeater (*Lichmera indistincta*), have been sighted in Bali, and brush turkeys (Megapodiidae) did, in fact, extend westwards as far as the Andaman Islands. Perhaps a more apt term might be Wallace's 'zone of transition' for this area of mixing: the name Wallacea has been used for the whole area between Wallace's original boundary, and 'Lydekker's Line', immediately west of New Guinea, which marks the easternmost limit of Asian influence.

During the glacial advances of the Ice Age, when much of the planet's water was stored in ice sheets and glaciers, ocean levels were up to 120 metres (390 ft) lower than today, and both Asia and Australia were united – as continuous land masses – with what are now islands on their respective continental shelves. However, the deep water between those two large masses was, for over 50 million years, a barrier that kept the flora and fauna of Australia separated from those of Asia. Wallacea includes those islands that were not recently connected by dry land to either of these two continental masses, and thus were populated by organisms capable of crossing the straits between islands; they therefore had arrivals from both the east and west. All these notions fit well with the modern theory of plate tectonics, which claims that the Australian plate, a part of the ancient supercontinent of Gondwana, has steadily moved northwards – following Gondwana's fracturing – for several tens of millions of years. The archipelago of the East Indies was formed by the pushing up of material as Australia collided with the Asian plate. The northward movement continues at about 7 cm ($2^3/_4$ in.)

per year. As the distance between the two plates narrowed, the organisms from Asia and Australia spread into this zone of transition. The result is that Wallacea contains a mixture of plant and animal species with both Asian and Australian affinities.

In fact Wallace did seem to understand the somewhat 'fuzzy' nature of the transition, for he included in his *The Malay Archipelago* – a number of tables showing the increase in the number of Australian birds, and the decrease in Javanese species, on moving eastwards through the archipelago from island to island (*MA*, chap. XIV).

	In Lombok	In Flores	In Timor
Javan birds	33	23	11
Closely allied to Javan birds	1	5	6
Total	34	28	17
Australian birds	4	5	10
Closely allied to Australian birds	3	9	26
Total	7	14	36

In noticing both contrasts and similarities between the many islands of the archipelago, and showing the magnitude of those similarities *quantitatively*, Wallace was an important innovator.

The Malay Archipelago, Wallace's best-known work from this period, is in part a travelogue but is also a remarkably detailed survey of the physical geography, plants, animals and anthropology of the East Indies – from Singapore and Sumatra in the west to the islands off New Guinea in the east. The book's subtitle gives a clue to the reason for its popularity, its integrative approach to humanity and its links to its environment: *The Land of the Orang-utan and the Bird of Paradise. A Narrative of Travel with Studies of Man and Nature.* Part of its appeal was its striking series of woodcuts, made from Wallace's sketches, specimens and photographs, by leading artists including Thomas Baines, Walter Hood Fitch, John Gerrard Keulemans, E. W.

Robinson, Joseph Wolf and T. W. Wood. It was the most successful of Wallace's books, and has seldom been out of print.

Another important piece of fall-out from the Asian journeyings appeared seven years later and further developed the sub-discipline of biogeography. This was *The Geographical Distribution of Animals; with a Study of the Relations of Living and Extinct Faunas as Elucidating the Past Changes of the Earth's Surface* (1876). As the title implies, this substantial work, building on his earlier article of 1863, discusses the distribution of organisms in *both time and space*. Moreover, it links evolutionary mechanisms with changes in the Earth's form. Wallace emphasized that evolution of plants and animals takes place against a backdrop of fluctuating sea levels, mountain building and changing climates.

In 1880 there appeared another highly integrative volume: as its predecessors had, it depended heavily on the East Indian Archipelago, but it painted a wide canvas. It was *Island Life: Or, the Phenomena and Causes of Insular Faunas and Floras*. Island biogeography, the study of the occurrence and distribution of plants and animals on remote (and not so remote) islands, has been an important theme in science ever since. (Darwin too emphasized the special nature of island biotas throughout *On the Origin of Species*, and Wallace acknowledged his contribution to island natural history freely in *Island Life*.) There can be distinguished *oceanic* islands, islands that have emerged from the sea through volcanic activity or coral growth (for example, the Azores, Bermuda, Galapagos and St Helena), and *continental* islands (like Britain, Ireland and some of the islands of the Malay Archipelago, such as Borneo) that were once part of a major land mass but have been separated from it by earth movement, or sea-level rise. The organisms inhabiting the former must have at some time either made the journey thither (for example, blown by the wind, floating on the ocean or hitch-hiking among the feathers of a sea-bird) or have evolved from, or been descended from, such creatures. The plants and animals of continental islands, on the other hand, are usually strongly similar to those of the land mass from which they have been separated (see earlier in this chapter). Moreover, the geology of the two island categories is very different: while remote, oceanic islands are built of (geologically) relatively recent lavas and coral limestones, continental islands often have the older, sometimes much folded and tilted rocks of the great continental masses.

Wallace spent the five decades following his return from Asia defending and popularizing, and elaborating, the theory of evolution through natural selection. He worked on an enormous variety of subjects, writing nearly 1,000 publications, including 22 books. He was never able to obtain salaried employment, living mainly from the rather sporadic income from his books (although he was an examiner for physical geography, setting and marking exam papers in this subject for two decades).

After Darwin's death in 1882 – Wallace acted as a pall-bearer at the funeral in Westminster Abbey – Wallace was, with the exception of T. H. Huxley, the only survivor of the early group of advocates of evolutionary ideas, and he saw it as his responsibility to promote them. It was partly with this in view, but also, as he always was impecunious, to earn some money, that he undertook a tour of the USA in 1886–7. He also wished to see the plants and animals of another major region of the world and to meet those Americans who had similar views to his, not only on evolution but on spiritualism and 'Owenism'. He lectured in New York, Boston and Washington. As an advocate of women's rights and emancipation, and with his rather progressive views, he was particularly interested in the all-female Vassar College. He visited Harvard and Yale, and met botanist Asa Gray. (It had been a fragment of a letter from Darwin to Asa that constituted a part of the Wallace–Darwin Linnean Society presentation in 1858.) On the whole, the visit was a success. Wallace knew he was an indifferent speaker and, in fact, a Boston newspaper even described him as 'a master of condensed statement' rather than an orator.[7] As he travelled, usually by train, in hesitating stages across America, he was able to botanize in forests and deserts and in the Rocky Mountains. Towards the latter part of the trek, the paid lecturing dried up from time to time, but he was not too discouraged. His goal was San Francisco, where his brother John, with whom he had surveyed in his youth, was living with his family – they had not met since Alfred had departed for the Amazon, John leaving for the goldfields of California. He also visited – as so many millions have, before and since – Yosemite and Niagara.

Particularly important around this stage of his life, as it collected together many of his ideas on evolution into a coherent whole, was his book *Darwinism*, first published in 1889. The lectures he gave in North America (he visited Canada on his return journey) provided an important stimulus for the contents of this publication. As he said,

> Many of my correspondents, as well as persons I met in America, told me they did not understand Darwin's 'Origin of Species', but they did understand my lecture on 'Darwinism'; and it therefore occurred to me that a popular exposition of the subject might be useful, not only as enabling the general reader to understand Darwin, but also to serve as an answer to the articles and books professing to disprove the theory of natural selection (*Life*, II, 201).

The title was also a tribute to Charles Darwin himself, the co-originator of the concept. After its first appearance in 1889, *Darwinism* was reprinted, sometimes with minor changes and corrections, over the next two decades. In some ways, it reflects the structure of *On the Origin of Species*, and Darwin's work is quoted frequently. Two early chapters are entitled 'The Struggle for Existence' (Chapter Two) and 'The Variability of Species in a State of Nature' (Chapter Three). Then, as in Darwin's original work, there is a discussion of the 'Variation of Domesticated

Travelling by train (through Utah) on the American lecture tour, as illustrated in Wallace's *My Life* (1905).

Animals and Cultivated Plants' (Chapter Four). Subsequently, the essential components of the evolutionary theory are pulled together in 'Natural Selection by Variation and Survival of the Fittest' (Chapter Five). Following Darwin's *On the Origin* model, 'Difficulties and Objections' are then dealt with (Chapter Six). Later chapters tackle geographical distributions (Chapter Twelve) and the geological evidence for evolution (Chapter Thirteen). But although aspects of the general plan follow *On the Origin*, as does much of the argument, the book should not be said to be that earlier work brought up to date. It very much has the stamp of Wallace upon it. It gives more emphasis to quantitative evidence, and there is also an emphasis on heredity.

Wallace was particularly expert on the colouration of animals, and in *Darwinism* he gave a whole series of examples of concealing or cryptic colouration – popularly called camouflage or disguise ('You can't see me'), warning colouration ('Look out! I'm dangerous') and mimicry ('I look like something that might be dangerous: you can't be sure, so avoid me') (*Darwinism*, chapters Eight, Nine, Ten and Eleven). Chapters Eight to Eleven of the work make especial reference to his work in the Malay Archipelago. One analysis runs as follows:

> In the arctic regions there are a number of animals which are wholly white all the year round, or which only turn white in winter. Among the former are the polar bear, the American polar hare, the snowy owl and the Greenland falcon; among the latter the arctic fox, the arctic hare, the ermine and the ptarmigan. Those which are permanently white remain among the snow nearly all the year round, while those which change colour inhabit regions that are free from snow in summer. The obvious explanation of this style of coloration is, that it is protective, serving to conceal herbivorous species from their enemies, and enable carnivores to approach their prey unperceived (*Darwinism*, chap. VIII).

Wallace allowed that there were alternative explanations: for example, that white colouration in itself reduced the loss of heat from the body; and that there was some direct effect on the creature of the predominantly white surroundings. Although he accedes that there is some possibility that at least the former may have some merit, he presumes that the main driving force is natural selection acting to eliminate the more conspicuous individuals from the population. A conspicuous carnivore would starve; in a prey species, conspicuousness would render it more liable to be eaten by predators. In either case, the creature concerned would be eliminated from the population.

Wallace gave a number of other instances of the same general theme. The predominance of grey-brown creatures in the deserts of the world; the occurrence of green birds in tropical forests, and of 'dusky colours' among nocturnal organisms. In addition,

> marine organisms . . . of larger size . . . [that] either occasionally or habitually float on the surface, are beautifully tinged with blue above, thus harmonising with the colour of the sea as seen hovering birds; while they are white below, and are thus invisible as seen by enemies beneath the surface (*Darwinism*, chap. VIII).

Even more elaborate concealment is effected by organisms, particularly insects, which actually resemble a particular object in their environments; some caterpillars merge with the leaves of their food-plant, and stick insects can be almost invisible while motionless in particular settings.

> In India *Kallima inacchis*, and in the larger Malay islands *K. paralekta*, are very common. They are rather large and showy butterflies, orange and bluish on the upper side, and with a very rapid flight, and frequenting dry forests. Their habit is to settle always where there is some dead or decaying

foliage, and the shape and colour of the wings (on the under surface), together with the attitude of the insect, is such as to produce an absolutely perfect imitation of a dead leaf. This is effected by the butterfly always settling on a twig, with the short tail of the hind wings just touching it and forming the leaf-stalk (*Darwinism*, chap. VIII).

Wallace also discusses 'warning coloration' – the exact opposite of the type of colouration described above because instead of serving to conceal the creatures that possess it, it renders the organism *more* conspicuous. It signifies the possession of 'weapons' such as fangs or stings, or the fact that the organism is inedible because it is poisonous or distasteful, or produces some offensive smell or has some other disagreeable characteristic. It has some distinctive signal that serves as a warning to potential attackers: this is usually some very conspicuous brilliant colouration, distinguishable from the protective colours of defenceless animals allied to them.

Wallace mentions the black-and-white fur and bushy white tail of the skunk that tell of its offensive nature; the bright colours of the day-flying European moth, the six-spot burnet; the brilliant yellow and black of cinnabar moth caterpillars; the bright red or yellow and black spots on ladybirds – all signify a distasteful nature. Predators associate these colours with toxic, disagreeable effects and avoid them. He summarized the situation as follows:

There are caterpillars which seem coloured on purpose to be conspicuous, and . . . they [may] have another type of protection . . . such as a disagreeable odour or taste. If they are thus protected . . . the majority of birds will never eat them . . . To get the full benefit of this protection they should be easily recognised, should have some outward character by which birds would soon learn to know them and let them alone.[8]

Were the birds unable to tell the 'eatable' from the 'inedible' by some sign, the unpleasant taste or toxicity would be to no avail. Birds could not determine the disagreeableness of their prey until they had seized and tasted (and killed) them. Natural selection in the case of organisms with 'warning' colouration would seem to be working on two groups of characteristics at once – their colour and appearance as well as the toxins within the body.

Finally, we may return to the subject of mimicry, in which Wallace was especially interested, although the early development of the idea was by H. W. Bates, with whom he had travelled in South America. There exist, particularly in the tropics, species of butterflies that are both conspicuously coloured and distasteful. But in the same regions there are other species, of completely different families, not so protected, that have come to resemble them very closely. Natural selection has so worked as to remove from the population of the latter those that differ most from the unpalatable species, encouraging variants that resemble it, passing their characteristics to their progeny.

Darwinism also gives instances of similar phenomena in other groups: a Philippines grasshopper that mimics a distasteful ladybird; harmless snakes from tropical America that imitate highly poisonous reptiles. An example that may be familiar to readers in temperate regions is the manner in which harmless hoverflies mimic the colouration of bees and wasps that bear an unpleasant sting. Ecology as a discipline was not well developed in Wallace's day, but in a host of ways, he used the concept of natural selection to explain the complex relations that exist between the organisms.

In 1859, in *On the Origin*, Darwin made little reference to humanity; *The Descent of Man* appeared in 1871. Wallace, however, in *Darwinism*, compares the bodily structure, particularly the brains, of the great apes with those of humans, coming to a clearly evolutionary conclusion:

The facts now very briefly summarised amount almost to a demonstration that man, in his bodily structure, has been derived from the lower animals, of which he is the culminating development (*Darwinism*, chap. xv).

The phrase 'culminating development' is interesting: it implies that the arrival of humans on the planet can be seen as the end point, almost the 'goal' of evolution. He goes on to describe the astounding mental, moral and intellectual development of humans. Very close to the end of the book he concludes that there exist

a number of mental faculties which either do not exist at all or exist in a very rudimentary condition in savages, but appear almost suddenly and in perfect development in the higher civilised races. These same faculties are further distinguished by their sporadic character, being well developed only in a very small proportion of the community . . . Each of these characteristics is totally inconsistent with any action of the law of natural selection in the production of [these] faculties . . . and the facts, taken in their entirety, compel us to recognise some origin for them wholly distinct from that which has served to account for the animal characteristics – whether bodily or mental – of man (*Darwinism*, chap. xv).

These ideas – that evolution can be seen as *teleological* or trending towards a goal or end-point, and that in the evolution of the mental capacities of humans we must look elsewhere than the mechanism of natural selection – were felt to be heretical to some of Wallace's scientific contemporaries (Darwin despaired at the notion) just as they are also anathema to many modern thinkers. They are discussed further in the next chapter.

6

The Radical and the Heretic

Wallace was 'radicalized' in his teenage years while living in London, and in the mechanics' institutes of South Wales and the Welsh borderlands. Throughout his life, he held what would now be described as 'somewhat left of centre' political views, notwithstanding his wish for the approval of the scientific establishment and his admiration for the country gentleman's way of life. (When, relatively late in his life, he owned his own home, he enjoyed gardening – an activity he shared with his wife.) He felt that he understood the working man following his days in a building firm in London, the rural peasant and smallholder after several years of land-surveying in Wales and the Welsh Borders, and the indigenous peoples of Asia and South America after his long years of travel and exploration in those regions.

However, Alfred Russel Wallace was very much of his own time, and his ambivalence in matters of race is apparent in the following rather lengthy quotation (from a letter to his boyhood friend George Silk).

[The] Malays speak . . . a curious half intelligible dialect, – Mahometans but retaining many pagan customs & superstitions. They are very ignorant, very lazy, & live absolutely on *rice* alone, thriving upon it however just as the Irish do or did on potatoes. They were a bad lot a few years ago, but the Dutch have brought them into order by their admirable system of supervision and government.

. . .

Nothing is worse & more absurd than the sneering prejudiced tone in which almost all English writers speak of the Dutch Government in the East – It has never been worse than ours have been, & is *now* much better; & what is greatly to their credit & not generally known, they take nearly the same pains to establish order & good government in those islands & possessions wh. are an annual loss to them, as in those which yield a revenue. I am convinced that their system is *right* & ours *wrong* in principle, – though of course in the practical working there may be & must be defects, & among the dutch [*sic*] themselves, both in Europe & India [the East Indies], there is a strong party against the present system, but they are mostly merchants & planters, who want to get trade & commerce of the country made free, wh. in my opinion would be an act of suicidal madness, & would moreover *injure* instead of benefiting the natives.

Personally, I do not much like the dutch out here, or the dutch officials: – but I cannot help bearing witness to the excellence of their government of native races, gentle yet firm, respecting their manners, customs & prejudices, yet introducing everywhere European law, order & industry.[1]

Few Western observers, working as scientists in a developing country today, would write in such outspoken terms, even in the privacy of a personal letter to a close friend. Yet the extract perhaps warrants some careful analysis.

Wallace assumes that 'European law, order and industry' are superior to the cultures of the indigenous people of Southeast Asia and has something of a disdain for the way of life of the Malays (he uses words and phrases such as: 'half intelligible', 'ignorant', 'lazy', 'a bad lot') and also, to some extent, by implication, the Irish. He is frank in his dislike of the Dutch. And yet he is extremely critical of the English colonial administrators, admiring the firm, gentle paternalism of the Dutch. He approves of the way in which local traditions and customs are allowed to continue and their 'admirable system of supervision and government', along with the way in which a benign economic policy provided careful governance both of areas of economic promise and those without. He has little time for the merchants and plantation owners who seek mainly to promote their own economic interests. In short, Wallace sees the people of the Archipelago through the lens of his own time – that of Victorian imperialism – but with an enlightened eye.

There is, in fact, a certain comparable ambivalence that runs through much of Wallace's thinking on social issues. One biographer put it as follows:

> Wallace's socialism was a confusing blend of government intercession and laissez-faire inactivity. At times he argued for more government intrusion, usually when he did not think that changes would come about naturally as a result of biological or cultural evolution. By contrast, in an analysis similar to those of his ideological mentor [social theorist Herbert Spencer], Wallace argued that bureaucratic mediation disturbed the natural flow of evolution that should ultimately drive society to an ultimate government-free state.[2]

As with much else, Wallace adopted an evolutionary approach to his social thinking. In a paper published in 1864, he argued that although organic evolution as a whole had been driven by natural selection and the survival of the fittest, 'in man as we now behold him it is different.' Thinking back to his experience of the indigenous peoples of South America and the Malay Archipelago, he argued that even among 'primitive' or 'savage' communities, 'the want of perfect limbs or other organs' does not have the same effect as in animals. Individuals that are weaker, smaller or possess some other disadvantage do not suffer the same penalty as in the animal kingdom. He went on:

> In proportion as these physical characteristics become of less importance, mental and moral qualities will have increasing influence on the well-being of the race. Capacity for acting in concert, for protection and for the acquisition of food and shelter; sympathy, which leads all in turn to assist each other; the sense of right, which checks depredations upon our fellows; the decrease of the combative and destructive propensities; self-restraint in present appetites; and that intelligent foresight which prepares for the future, are all qualities that from their earliest appearance must have been for the benefit of each community, and would, therefore, have become the subjects of 'natural selection'. For it is evident that such qualities would be for the well-being of man; would guard him against external enemies, against internal dissensions, and against the effects of inclement seasons and impending famine, more surely than could any merely physical modification. Tribes in which such mental and moral qualities were predominant would have an advantage in the struggle for existence over other tribes in which they were less developed, would live and maintain their numbers, while the others would decrease and finally succumb.[3]

Wallace was profoundly influenced by Herbert Spencer, believing that his work synthesized the totality of human knowledge about the universe 'into one great system of evolution everywhere conforming to the same general principles'. Both thus thought that evolution, however caused, and whether of organisms or of human society, was teleological in nature – that is, it represented a trend in a definite direction towards an end purpose or goal. (This notion, accepted by some late Victorians, is deplored by many modern scientists and philosophers, but by no means all.) Wallace believed that the physical form of humans had developed into a body 'that was the highest type possible on earth', although he did not believe that civilization or society had reached its highest state. He felt that societies tended to progress (or evolve) towards the goal of a state where each person could fulfil their purpose without harming others. He asked, rhetorically,

> What is this ideally perfect social state towards which mankind ever has been, and still is tending? Our best thinkers maintain that it is a state of individual freedom and self-government, rendered possible by the equal development and just balance of the intellectual, moral and physical parts of our nature (*MA*, chap. XI).

The utopianism of Wallace seemed to perceive humanity evolving towards a state of perfection (he occasionally admitted that this might never actually be attainable). He believed that it was not inappropriate for governments occasionally to give society a 'nudge' in what he perceived to be the right direction.

Of his many social campaigns, one of the most striking was his advocacy of the nationalization of land. He entitled a book *Land Nationalisation*, and was founding president of the Land Nationalisation Society; he addressed meetings of the Society, and wrote a series of 'tracts' expounding its beliefs. In these it was argued that no one can have real ownership of land, as land is permanent, but all human life is transient. Landowners have an unequal share of the wealth and power that proprietorship of land conveys. No one should be permitted to hold more than a life interest in land.

This particular piece of utopianism was sometimes carried to extreme lengths:

Now, an essential part of our scheme of Land Nationalisation is, that every man can *claim as a right* (once in his life) to have such a piece of land allotted to him, at its fair agricultural value; and further he shall not be obliged to take any piece of land however unsuitable it may be to him, but he shall be able to choose a piece wherever most convenient to himself, the only limit being that it must *adjoin some public road* . . . The principle, we maintain is that it should be the birthright of every British subject to have the use and enjoyment of a portion of his native land, with no unnecessary restrictions on that enjoyment other than that implied by the equal right of others.

. . .

The land would be cultivated and improved in his spare time . . . He could grow vegetables, or fruit, or flowers, or keep poultry or pigs . . .[4]

Wallace, the aspirant country gentleman, saw individuals building 'small cottages' on their land allocation. In 1900–1901, along with a few of his like-minded socialist colleagues, he even drafted a formal proposal for the purchase and development of a cooperative land scheme; they were hoping to purchase some 300 acres [120 ha] or so, somewhere in England, and to develop it in accordance with Wallace's theories of land ownership and management. Preliminary enquiries were also made about establishing such a colony in Africa. Neither scheme ever came to fruition. In any case, such utopian schemes could not have survived into the twentieth century when populations increased dramatically, and as the world became increasingly technological. Needless to say, advocating the nationalization of land (the holdings of the Church of England were not considered exempt) did not go down well with some of the figures in the British Establishment of the day.

There are comparisons between Wallace's devotion to land nationalization and the fervour with which he argued against vaccination, although in the latter case he *opposed* government intervention. Nothing existed in nature that did not have a purpose, he suggested, and argued on the basis of the assumption that humanity lived in society in a 'natural', equilibrial state, and government interference generally disturbed the 'innate harmony of nature', of the *harmonia naturae*.

Wallace undertook extensive statistical analysis attempting to show that not only did vaccination fail to prevent disease, it actually increased the number of deaths because of the haphazard doses and the crude methods by which inoculations were administered. In a booklet addressed 'To Members of Parliament and Others' and entitled *Forty-five Years of Registration Statistics, Proving Vaccination to Be Both Useless and Dangerous* (1885), he attempts a rigorous analysis, in both graphical and tabular form, of the Registrar-General's reports from 1838 to 1882. Below is one of Wallace's tables exactly as he published it.

ANNUAL DEATHS IN ENGLAND PER MILLION LIVING

Average of 5 years	1850–4	1855–9	1860–4	1865–9	1870–4	1875–9	1878–80
Small-pox	279	199	191	148	433	82	40
Syphilis	37	51	64	82	81	86	84
Cancer	302	327	369	404	442	493	510
Tabes Mesenterica	265	261	272	316	299	330	341
Pyaemia, &c	20	18	24	23	29	39	40
Skin Disease	12	15	16	17	18	23	22
Totals	636	672	745	842	869	971	997
Progressive Increase	0	36	109	206	233	335	361

(Readers should note that the figures are *averages*, for five-year periods, per million people living for each individual cause of death. The absolute totals are therefore not necessarily the sum of these means. The overlap in the last column is in the table in the original pamphlet.)

Wallace commented as follows:

We here see a constant increase in the mortality from each of these diseases, an increase which in the sum of them is steady and continuous. It is true, we have not, and cannot have, direct proof that vaccination is the sole cause of this increase, but we have good reason to believe that it is the chief cause . . . since it directly inoculates infants and adults, on an enormous scale, with whatever blood-disease may exist unsuspected in the system.

Wallace argued that vaccination had been 'encouraged' from 1838 to 1853, had been 'compulsory' from then until 1867, and actually been subject to 'penal' sanctions from that time onwards. There had actually been an increase in the death-rate from smallpox immediately following the imposition of sanctions. Also, despite vaccination, the *overall* death-rate had increased following its introduction. Moreover, when he examined even longer-term trends, he deduced that the number of smallpox deaths was already falling before compulsory vaccination was introduced.

It is not difficult to criticize Wallace's arguments from the standpoint of the twenty-first century. There may have been problems with diagnosis; data collection was probably very imperfect in the early and middle decades of the nineteenth century. Wallace was not medically qualified, and indeed contemporary medical journals were vitriolic, mocking him for making absolutely basic errors. Nevertheless, he persisted doggedly. If anything, the vehemence of his arguments increased. Another booklet appeared in 1898, entitled *Vaccination a Delusion: Its Penal Enforcement a Crime. Proved by the Official Evidence in the Reports of the Royal Commission*. A copy of this was sent by Wallace to the former prime minister, William Gladstone, while other copies made their way into Parliament and were sufficiently influential for a bill to be presented allowing parents to object to the compulsory, or 'penal', vaccination of their children.[5] This legal situation still exists in many countries today.[6]

The modern view would be that Wallace was completely misguided. But one has to admire his persistence in pursuit of what he felt both to be right and in the interests of the common people, as well as his careful analysis, desire for a 'scientific' study of the data, and what we would now call an 'evidence-based' approach to social problems. And he was not completely naive: in a 1904 pamphlet he wrote – and those who are sceptical of the use of statistics in today's world would wholeheartedly agree – that 'the figures go increasing and decreasing so suddenly and so irregularly, that by taking only a few years at one period, and a few at another, you can show an increase or decrease according to what you want to prove.'

There are those who see the entire corpus of Wallace's work as an integrated whole: they would argue that all, or almost all, of his 1,000 or so publications can be arranged around a single theme, or a very limited number of themes. Certainly, he applied notions of evolution to both the natural world and to human society; he wrote about glaciation – the causes and effects of ice ages, or glacial epochs – feeling that environmental and climatic change might be one of the drivers of adaptation and evolution.[7] One can suggest that some of his thoughts on what might be described as 'astrobiology' or speculations about the possibility of the existence of life on other planets had a vaguely ecological or evolutionary thrust (these are discussed in Chapter Seven). But to link his flirtation with the 'pseudosciences' of phrenology (the idea that one could make certain deductions about an individual's character on the basis of the shape of his or her head) and mesmerism, with his evolutionary ideas, is perhaps more contrived. And then there is his embracing of spiritualism, a cause to which he leant his support for several decades, even though the very idea of it was ridiculed by many of his scientific friends. And why did he get involved with a dispute with the 'flat-Earthers'?

Perhaps clues can be found in his radicalism and his notions about teleology, the goal- or purpose-driven nature of the entire universe; his belief that in life, in human society and perhaps in the universe as a whole there was a trend towards 'development' and 'improvement'. There was also his devotion to the scientific approach – his belief that nothing, however bizarre, should be immune from investigation in a rigorous manner. However, his frequent naivety in the face of established opinion possibly suggests that there might be some psychological cause.

A book review written by Wallace for an 1869 issue of *Quarterly Review* (126, p. 392) expressed a certain puzzlement about the origin of the enlarged human brain, as well as the organs of speech and the manipulating hand, compared with those of the apes. 'In the brain of the lowest savages, and, as far as we know, of the prehistoric races we have an organ . . . little inferior in size and complexity' to those of modern, Western humans. He wondered, how could the brain have developed far beyond the requirements of its possessor? 'Natural selection could only have endowed the savage with a brain a little superior to that of the ape, but he actually possesses one but very little inferior to that of the average members of our learned scientists.' The socialist Wallace could not resist an opportunity to make a swipe at the scientific elites of his world!

There must be, he postulated, an 'Overruling Intelligence' that 'watched over' the laws of natural selection and evolution, 'directing' variations and their accumulation and ultimately producing 'an organization sufficiently perfect' to allow the 'indefinite advancement of our mental and moral nature'. Natural selection, he argued, could not possibly select for the needs of the future; there must be a guiding hand directing it. Mere chance variation was insufficient to propel the human brain and mind towards its destiny.

Wallace gave many other instances of what he felt was 'pre-selection'; for example,

Looking at it as a whole, the bird's wing seems to me to be, of all the mere mechanical organs of any living thing, that which most clearly implies the working out of a pre-conceived design in a new and apparently most complex and difficult manner to produce a marvellously successful result (*World of Life*, pp. 287–8).

He emphasized that the jointed, bony structure of the wings of birds had been reduced to a 'compact' minimum, the breast bone was enlarged to give increased power to the pectoral muscles, and that extremely light, elaborately structured, flexible feathers had evolved. There must have been some directionality, some guiding mechanism, that produced the coherent whole of a bird's wing, the complexity of a feather's structure and the power of flight. Something more than natural selection must have been responsible for the development of the birds' feathers and wings.

He also thought that the brilliance of butterflies' wings, covered with the tiniest of coloured scales, might be indicative of a similar 'pre-selection' process:

The wonderful metallic colours of so many butterflies are not caused by pigments but are 'interference colours' produced by striae [linear marks] on the surface of the scales. Of course, where eye-spots, fine lines or delicate shadings adorn the wings, each scale must have its own special colour, something like each small block in a mosaic picture.

. . .

As regards the effect of the shading and coloration of insects upon the higher animals, there is ample evidence . . . that the markings and tints of insects often resemble their environment in a remarkable manner, and that this resemblance is protective. The eye-like markings, either on the upper or under surfaces, are often seen to be imitations of the eyes of vertebrates, when at rest, and this also is protective. The brilliant metallic or phosphorescent colours on the wings of butterflies may serve to distract enemies from attacking a vital part, or, in the smaller species may alarm the enemy by a sudden change of position. But while the colours are undoubtedly useful, the mode of producing them [by means of myriads of minute scales covering the wings] seems unnecessarily elaborate, and adds a greater difficulty in the way of any mechanical or chemical conception of their production (*World of Life*, pp. 302–4).

Wallace wrote extensively about both concealing and warning colouration (see Chapter Five), and knew what he was talking about. His position was that both could well be the result of natural selection. The uncannily leaflike appearance of some insects, caused by the arrangement of millions of tiny scales rather than simply by pigments, and the dazzlingly realistic flashing of two bright 'eyes' when a butterfly opened its wings were clearly evolutionary adaptations: both would allow the insect to survive and pass on its characteristics to the next generation. But the quite extraordinary brilliance of the colours – for example seen in certain specimens that he collected in the Malay Archipelago – and the fact that these were produced by the interplay of light with the surfaces of millions of scales, and not just from pigmentation, seemed to imply some almost Lamarckian guiding mechanism.

In fact, taking things to their logical conclusion, it would not be too great a generalization to say that Wallace believed that the 'ultimate purpose' of nature, and of evolution, was the development of the human spirit. It was this strand of evolution that was connected with the social development of humanity mentioned above.[8]

When he read of Wallace's teleological approach, Darwin uttered a 'groan' (his word) at the idea that there was a powerful directionality of evolution. The notion that evolution had a purpose or ultimate goal was abhorrent to him, and despite his enormous respect for much of Wallace's work, Darwin did not think that the history either of the natural world or of humankind had a single straight arrow running through it.

We have seen that from his teenage years there was a certain contrarianism in Wallace's writings and thought: from his days attending (and giving) lectures in mechanics' institutes and at the Hall of Science, he was prepared to question widely held views. He was at the beck and call of Welsh Borders landowners in rural Bedfordshire as a surveyor, but in his own mind deplored both the Enclosure movement that robbed many country people of their birthright and the whole notion of a Church supported by tithes. In the East Indies, he had no great affection for the Dutch colonial administrators, but he admired many aspects of their enlightened regime, which respected the customs of the local people. He was unhappy in the early years of his career with a creationist explanation of life's diversity and moved gradually towards the evolutionary stance. Wallace was willing to embrace wild, unpopular ideas, to 'give them a chance' and to subject them to serious scientific study. What was thought of as extraordinary, hotly disputed or fraudulent in one age might be accepted as a natural phenomenon in the next. To a person who lived in the tropics, he argued, the notion of ice and snow might appear absurd. In the eighteenth century, only the gullible or superstitious would have believed in the telegrams and photographs of the nineteenth.

Every idea was worthy, therefore, of sensible, serious scientific investigation and scrutiny. The variations in dozens of butterfly specimens collected in the East Indies were to be detailed and catalogued. Statistics on death-rates and vaccinations should be rigorously analysed. Why not the phenomena of mesmerism, phrenology and spiritualism?

The details of Alfred Russel Wallace's dalliances with these ideas have been frequently described (and disputed); for example, there is evidence that he first encountered phrenology and mesmerism in

Leicester as a very young man. Only a few aspects and incidents can be detailed here.

The fundamental notions of phrenology were introduced in the late eighteenth century. It was argued by an Austrian medical doctor, Franz Joseph Gall, that the mind is the sum total of mental processes localized in specific areas of the brain – the larger the particular brain area, the more highly developed the specific mental process associated with it. He argued that, because the skull is plastic in young infants, when it formed and ossified around the brain it would conform to the configuration of the brain beneath, the bumps and depressions reflecting the individual's mental faculties. Phrenology was assimilated by some members of the medical profession, giving it the cachet of respectability in the eyes of some levels of society. Indeed, when Captain Robert FitzRoy was interviewing the young Darwin for his position aboard HMS *Beagle* in 1831, he was profoundly influenced by the shape of the young naturalist's head! Darwin himself, like many others, thought the whole business was complete nonsense.

After about 1840 phrenology lost credibility in the scientific community, although advocates lingered among the working classes – particularly, it is asserted, in the more radical sections of the proletariat. Wallace first read about phrenology in 1844, attended public lectures on the subject and had his own head read phrenologically. He also wrote a very short letter on mesmerism to the journal *The Critic* when he was 22 (in 1845).

He describes, in his autobiography, incidents that blended his commitment to an experimental, scientific approach (which perhaps can even be traced back to his 'pebbles in the water' experiment in early childhood; see Chapter One) with his interests in both phrenology and mesmerism. The latter can be defined as the attempt to exert power or control over a person's (or an animal's) personality or behaviour, as in hypnosis or suggestion. Wallace tried an experiment on a young person while he was at the school in Leicester, in 1844.

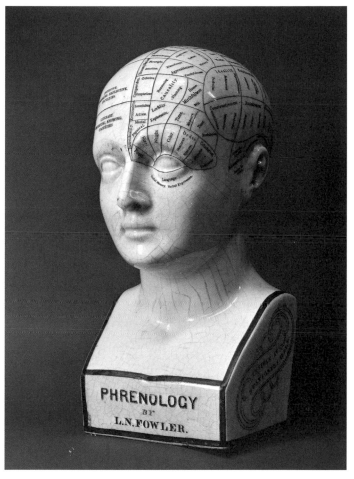

Ceramic phrenology head.

Giving him a glass of water and telling him it was wine or brandy, he would drink it and soon show all the signs of intoxication, while if I told him his shirt was on fire he would strip himself naked to get it off. I also found he had community of sensation with myself when in the trance. If I held his hand he tasted whatever I put in my mouth . . . and if another person . . . pricked or pinched me . . . he instantly felt the same sensation. . . .

In like manner . . . a light could be flashed on his eyes or a pistol fired behind his head without his showing the slightest sign of having seen or heard anything. More curious still was the taking away the memory so completely that he could not tell his own name, and would adopt whatever name was suggested to him, and perhaps remark how stupid he was to have forgotten it (*Life*, 1, 234).

On another occasion, with a phrenological bust at his disposal, Wallace claimed that he put a person in a trance and with the bust on the table behind him, touched several of the organs, the position of which was easy to determine. After a few seconds, so Wallace stated, the subject would change his attitude and facial expression in correspondence with the organ excited (*Life*, 1, 235–6).

The precise origin of these tales is a little obscure, but at least they seem to suggest an experimental, participatory, observational approach to every phenomenon that Wallace regarded as worthy of serious scientific enquiry.

Wallace probably first came across ideas of spiritualism, or something akin to it – spiritualism being defined as a belief that the spirits of the dead are able to communicate with the living – during his travels among the indigenous peoples of South America and Asia. In his notes made in the East are a number of references to ghouls or ghosts. In some forms of spiritualism, the afterlife was often seen not as static, but as places where spirits continued to evolve and develop; it may have been this that attracted Wallace – it was compatible with his ideas of continuous change and improvement.

The origins of the modern spiritualist movement are often given as 31 March 1848, when two sisters from New York, Margaret and Kate Fox, claimed to communicate with spirits of the dead through 'rapping noises'. (Four decades later they confessed that the affair had been a hoax, the rapping and popping noises produced by the sisters' ability to generate clicks with the knuckles in their toes.) The movement swept the USA and crossed the Atlantic. Spiritualism was probably at its height in the years following 1850, and one estimate has it that there were 8 million adherents in the USA alone. The words 'telepathy' and 'medium' entered the language; the latter was the name given to a person who claimed to be an intermediary between the spirits and their earthbound disciples.

The movement became quite popular in Britain, especially among women, and seances were held among fashionable people in London. Popular songs were written about the rappings, and although many thought the whole business complete nonsense, a number of intelligent and well-educated individuals allied themselves with the cause at least temporarily: these included writers Anthony Trollope and William Makepeace Thackeray; physicists Sir William Crookes and Lord Rayleigh; mathematician Augustus De Morgan; the science writer Mary Somerville; and several well-known psychologists and physiologists. Most (but not all) of these people sought not to challenge the claims of the spiritualists, but to adopt a scientific approach to seeking an explanation of phenomena that seemed to them to have some basis in reality. At seances, usually held in darkened rooms, the dead appeared to communicate with the living through writing that appeared on slates, laden tables moving about the room and flowers arriving from nowhere. Bells rang, apparently without human intervention, and musical instruments played themselves. There are even tales of levitation and of individuals (often young and female) appearing and disappearing.

Wallace had attended his first seance in 1865, published on the subject within a few months, and was drawn into the dispute on the side of the spiritualists. He continued to write and speak on the subject quite extensively. Like that of a number of other 'men of science', his approach was that these phenomena might have a rational explanation and deserved to be investigated in a thorough and logical way. He attended many sessions describing the strange events that occurred in some detail. His interest was long-lasting: he was attending seances in London in the 1860s, suggesting that the British Association for the Advancement of Science should look into the matter; he was still attending seances in 1886, sometimes on the same day as collecting animal and plant specimens and while giving public lectures on Darwinism during a visit to the USA. His *Miracles and Modern Spiritualism* was published in 1875, a second edition appeared on 1881, and an expanded third one in 1896.[9]

A distinguished historian of science, James Moore, has added another dimension to the discussion of Wallace's extraordinary relationship with spiritualism. He pointed out that when Wallace returned from Asia, he was desperate to get married and settle down (see Chapter Five); he became engaged, and then his fiancée jilted him. Wallace was extremely upset and possibly craved female company, which he may have found in spiritualist sessions. After his mother – with whom, along with his sister, he had attended seances – died, he became further depressed. In 1874 a well-known medium called Mrs Guppy, née Miss Nicholl, allegedly managed to get his mother's image to appear on a photographic plate. Moore suggested that it was at these times of difficulty that he surrounded himself with 'dotty women', eschewing the (almost exclusively male) society of his brother scientists.

Thomas Henry Huxley, who had so championed evolutionary ideas, professed to be completely uninterested when Wallace suggested a thorough scientific investigation. Other colleagues were disappointed and shocked that Wallace, whose scientific work

Frederick Hudson's 'spirit photograph' of 'Alfred Russel Wallace, F.R.G.S., and his mother', from Georgiana Houghton's *Chronicles of the Photographs of Spiritual Beings* (1882). The book does not fully explain the circumstance in which this photograph was alleged to have been taken.

they respected, could have got involved with something they considered completely fraudulent. Fraud was, in fact, established to the satisfaction of a court in London in October 1876 when an American spiritualist, Henry Slade, was prosecuted under a section of a statute known as the Vagrancy Act of 1824, which was intended to deal with 'rogues and vagabonds' and to outlaw fortune-telling. Wallace, perhaps naively, gave evidence. At the trial, Slade was found guilty and was sentenced to three months in prison. However, Slade appealed on the grounds that the words 'by palmistry or otherwise' had been omitted from the original indictment. But before he could be arrested on a new summons, he had fled back to the USA.

There is another dispute that went on for much longer and caused Wallace even greater irritation. In January 1870, a Mr John Hampden placed an advertisement in the journal *Scientific Opinion* stating he was willing to deposit up to £500 in a wager that defied 'all the philosophers, divines, and scientific professors in the United Kingdom to prove the rotundity . . . of the world from Scripture, from reason, or from fact'. He went on to say that he would acknowledge that he had forfeited his deposit if his opponent were able to demonstrate to the satisfaction of a referee 'a convex railway, river, canal or lake'. Wallace was always short of money, and feeling that straightforward scientific observation and

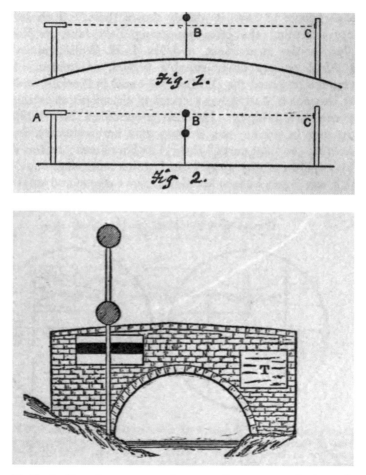

The 'Flat Earth' experiment, as conveyed across two illustrations in Wallace's *My Life*.

Wallace in 1869, from his autobiography, *My Life* (1905).

experiment would demonstrate the falsity of the flat-Earth cause, was drawn in. Unfortunately, and somewhat surprisingly, geologist Charles Lyell encouraged him. An experiment was set up on an absolutely straight 9.5-kilometre (6-mi.) stretch of the Old Bedford Level, a drainage canal in eastern England. Wallace set up a telescope, a disc and a black band exactly the same height above the water. He later wrote of the experiment,

> If the surface of the water is a perfectly straight line for six miles [10 km], then . . . the disc would be seen in the telescope projected on the black band; whereas, if the six-mile surface of the water is convexly curved the . . . disc would appear decidedly higher than the black band (*Life*, ii, 365–6).

The experiment took place on 5 March 1870, and Wallace was declared the winner by the referee; the results were published three weeks later in *The Field*. Hampden refused to accept the result and demanded his money back. Seemingly an unbalanced individual, Hampden then started to send scurrilous letters to several of the scientific societies of which Wallace was a member; he used phrases such as 'unprincipled blackguards', 'rogues and swindlers', 'convicted thief and swindler'. Poor Wallace, in a letter he wrote in May 1871, described Mr Hampden as 'half mad'. Hampden also made physical threats, such as this to Wallace's wife:

> Madam – if your infernal thief of a husband is brought home some day on a hurdle, with every bone in his head smashed to pulp, you will know the reason. Do you tell him from me he is a lying infernal thief, and as sure as his name is Wallace he never dies in his bed. You must be a miserable wretch to be obliged to live with a convicted felon. Do not think or let him think I have done with him (*Life*, II, 371).

Nor had he. The matter dragged on for over fifteen years. Hampden continued to deluge Wallace, his family and associates with letters, sometimes calling at his home. A series of civil actions and prosecutions followed, and Hampden spent some considerable time in prison. Eventually Wallace recovered the £500, but the cost of the legal actions, not to mention that of the original experiment, was far greater – to say nothing of the worry and wear and tear on his family. Ill fortune tormented Alfred Russel Wallace many times in his long life.

Wallace blamed himself for his lack of judgement; and this was not for the first or last time. Not only was he sometimes a poor judge of character, but he had an almost unquenchable belief that rigorous, careful scientific enquiry was the way to approach almost all problems. There was something almost wild, or heretic, about the way he thought and the manner in which he approached the world.

7

To the End of the Universe

Alfred Russel Wallace is best remembered for his biological work, much of which has an evolutionary thrust, and for his work on society, at least some of which can be linked to his evolutionary ideas. It is less well known that he held what he described as a 'deep interest' in astronomy for much of his life, and late in his career, he wrote two books in this field, which also discussed astronomy's biological and social implications. In 1903, ten years before his death, he published a book with the rather Victorian title *Man's Place in the Universe: A Study of the Results of Scientific Research in Relation to the Unity or Plurality of Worlds*. Four years later, in 1907, he produced a book with a narrower focus but a comparably long-winded title: *Is Mars Habitable? A Critical Examination of Professor Percival Lowell's Book 'Mars and Its Canals', with an Alternative Explanation*.

As a teenager, while surveying in the Bedfordshire countryside, he acquired a sextant and read a book on nautical astronomy he had borrowed from his brother. Wallace constructed a telescope through which he observed the craters of the Moon, the satellites of Jupiter and star clusters; he certainly made use of some basic navigational techniques while finding his way in remote areas of South America and Southeast Asia.

Throughout his career, Wallace had always taken a remarkably integrative approach: much of his writing was profoundly ecological in nature. In his work on the colouration of animals, he described the phenomenon of concealing colouration or camouflage perceptively, and his account of birds in Southeast Asia showed how the appearance, behaviour and habitat of bird species were interrelated. The whole idea of evolution through natural selection depends on the notion of a dialogue between an organism (or population, or group) and its environment. He appreciated that there existed an essential harmony in nature. To some extent, this included humanity, which Wallace frequently linked with the environment – something that he felt strongly should be preserved. His accounts of travels in both South America and Asia are littered with accounts of the manner in which the indigenous peoples used the resources and landscapes among which they lived, and how they were dependent upon them. Despite being a collector on a massive scale, he appreciated the importance of conservation. On the biological richness in the forests of the Malay Archipelago, he wrote,

> The modern naturalist . . . looks upon every species of animal and plant now living as the individual letters which go to make up one of the volumes of our earth's history; and, as a few lost letters may make a sentence unintelligible, so the extinction of the numerous forms of life which the progress of cultivation invariably entails will necessarily render obscure this invaluable record of the past.[1]

The above was a perceptive observation for 1863, at the height of Britain's imperial dominance. Later, when he argued in print for an extreme conservationist approach to the management of Epping Forest, he failed to be appointed to a position responsible for this important forest resource.[2]

It is unsurprising, therefore, that Wallace should continue his speculations about humanity's relationship with its environment by broadening his view – from humanity's relation to other forms of life and then on to his extensive commentaries about society and finally to humans' relationship with the entire cosmos.

We have already seen that Wallace believed that humans were unique: although he recognized that there were similarities between humans and the primates, he thought that there was a marked distinction, and that some other process beyond the natural selection mechanism was responsible for the development of the human mind, moral consciousness and complex societies.[3] There was, he maintained, a purposefulness, a directionality about evolution. Wallace believed in a 'purposeful' universe. For him, evolution inexorably led to the development of humans, who were capable of perfectibility of the mind and spirit.

Human beings, Wallace maintained, were the culmination, or end-point, of organic evolution. And some controlling Intelligence or Mind had produced the planet that had eventually led to the rise of humanity. Humans were, therefore, Wallace felt, unique and alone in the vast universe. And so, in much of his work, Alfred Russel Wallace was both teleological and anthropocentric: Man was the centre of everything – on the Earth and in the universe – and there was a special role for humanity in the 'chain of being'.

There were theological arguments in circulation mid-century that tended to emphasize this viewpoint. For example, William Whewell (1794–1866), Anglican priest, mathematician, poet, philosopher and polymath (he coined the word 'scientist'), wrote *Of the Plurality of Worlds* in 1853. In this he argued strongly against the existence of life on other worlds. He maintained that no proof existed that other stars had planets, and as some were binary stars, if they did have planets, conditions would be very different from those on Earth. As an Anglican priest, he was invested in the Christian doctrines of incarnation and redemption, which assumed the uniqueness of humanity. Wallace's philosophical and religious views differed greatly from those of Whewell, although both believed in some pattern or purpose in Life and the Universe. Other influences on Wallace included the work of astronomers Sir John Herschel (1792–1871) and Sir Joseph Norman Lockyer (1836–1920), both of whom suggested that the Sun (and therefore the Earth) was situated near the very centre of the Milky Way galaxy. It was this centrality, according the Wallace, that rendered the Earth suitable for life. In an article in 1903, he declaimed,

> But during the last quarter of the past century the rapidly increasing body of facts and observations leading to a more detailed and accurate knowledge of stars and stellar systems have thrown a new and somewhat unexpected light on this very interesting problem of our relation to the universe of which we form a part; and although these discoveries have, of course, no bearing upon the special theological dogmas of the Christian, or any other religion, they do tend to show our position in the material universe is special and probably unique, and that it is such as to lend support to the view . . . that the supreme end and purpose of this vast universe was the production and development of the living soul in the perishable body of man.[4]

There were also arguments based on the geological and fossil record that he felt supported this view:

> I . . . paid special attention to the problem of the measurement of geological time, and that of the mild climates and generally uniform conditions that had prevailed throughout all geological epochs; and on considering . . . the delicate balance of conditions required to maintain such uniformity, I become . . . convinced that the evidence was exceedingly strong against the . . . possibility of any other planet being inhabited.[5]

When Wallace was writing these things, all astronomical phenomena known at the time were usually seen as components of a single system, with the Sun in a more-or-less central position. This system was, it was assumed, held together through gravitational force.

Meanwhile, Percival Lowell (1855–1916), an American businessman, orientalist, mathematician and astronomer, had been thinking about the universe in a very different way. A wealthy Harvard graduate, he constructed an observatory near Flagstaff, Arizona – a location with clear skies and (at that time) a freedom from the distracting lights of a city. He concentrated his telescopes on the planets, particularly Venus and Mars. Although he did not discover Pluto, some of his observations prepared the way for its discovery, some years after his death.

Lowell was profoundly influenced by the writings of the Italian astronomer Giovanni Virginio Schiaparelli (1835–1910), who was the first to attempt to draw maps of Mars. He suggested that there existed dark areas, which he called *canali* in Italian, meaning 'channels'; the word however, was wrongly translated into English as 'canals' – and the idea persisted.

In the later years of the nineteenth century, and the first decade of the twentieth, Lowell viewed Mars extensively through his telescopes and made detailed drawings of what he believed to be the surface markings. He published his views in a series of books: *Mars* (1895), *Mars and Its Canals* (1906) and *Mars as the Abode of Life* (1908). It was these three works that, above all else, popularized the belief that Mars was inhabited by intelligent life forms.

Lowell included in these works a very detailed description of what he decided were the 'non-natural features' of Mars's surface, including an account of what he saw as linear features or 'canals' and 'oases' – the latter his term for the dark spots which he believed he could see at the points where these alleged dark lines intersected. He noted the manner in which the visibility of these features appeared to vary, depending on the Martian seasons. Lowell suggested that an advanced but desperate culture had built the canals to tap water from what he thought were Mars's polar ice caps, the only remaining source of water on an inexorably drying planet.

While these ideas excited the public enormously, the scientific community was extremely sceptical. Despite searching, many astronomers could not see these markings. In 1909 the 150-centimetre (60-in.) Mount Wilson Observatory telescope in southern California allowed close observation of Lowell's 'canals', and they were described as irregular, geological features, probably formed as the result of natural processes.[6]

Lowell's ideas on the existence of intelligent life on the planet Mars were, of course, complete anathema to Wallace. His claims of an anthropocentric universe implied the uniqueness of humanity, and the non-existence of any life beyond the Earth. Wallace argued that throughout the universe, the chemical elements would always behave in the same way; it followed, therefore, that life could only exist under conditions similar to those that had given rise to it on Earth and that assured its continual survival – among which are an appropriate atmosphere, the presence of water and a temperature between 0°c and 40°c (32°F and 104°F). These conditions, he said, would only exist on a planet of the approximate size of the Earth, with a similar orbit, around a sun of a similar size, and with the existence of a mild climate throughout geological time. 'It seems in the highest degree improbable,' he argued, 'that they can all [that is, that all these conditions could] again be found combined either in the solar system or even in the stellar universe.'[7] And if the Earth were the only inhabited planet in the universe, this could be seen either as an enormous coincidence, or that the Earth had been brought into existence for the purpose of the development of life and humanity. Moreover, Wallace asserted that humans are the result of an extremely long evolution, with various changes occurring under very special individual circumstances, and the likelihood of those circumstances existing elsewhere in the universe was infinitesimally small – thus the chance of any beings remotely

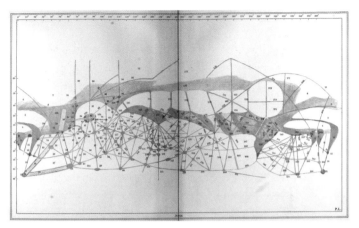

Percival Lowell's Martian map, from *Mars* (1895), plate XXIV.

similar to humans existing elsewhere is correspondingly minute.
Despite there being an enormous diversity of animal forms, he
felt that no other creature approached the intelligence or moral
consciousness of humans:

> If the physical or cosmical improbabilities as set forth in
> this volume are somewhere about a million to one, then the
> evolutionary improbabilities now urged cannot be considered
> to be less than perhaps a hundred millions to one; and the total
> chances against the evolution of man or an equivalent intellectual
> being, in any other planet, through the known laws of evolution,
> will be represented by a hundred millions [*sic*] of millions to one.[8]

In 1907, therefore, a year after the publication of Lowell's
Mars and Its Canals, Wallace launched his critique: a critique that
depended partly on his geocentrism and anthropocentrism (his
assertion that the Earth and humanity had central places in the
universe) and partly on Lowell's lack of solid evidence for the
presence of intelligent life on Mars. Wallace the scientist maintained

Wallace in 1895, from the occult review *Borderland*.

that there was no solid proof of the existence of the canals, or the beings that had created them: the whole edifice was based on an absurd theory. In any case, Mars was too cold, there was no water, and it was therefore 'irresistible that animal life, especially in its higher forms, cannot exist on the planet'.

Wallace was misguided in his assertion that the Earth was the centre of the universe; it is now understood that the Sun has a rather peripheral position in relation to the Milky Way galaxy, and there exist millions of other galaxies in an expanding universe; yet in over a hundred years since he wrote *Man's Place in the Universe*, no irrefutable proof of the existence of life away from the Earth has been forthcoming. Along the way, however, in seeking some sort of union between cosmology and biology, he anticipated modern thinkers and the development of astrobiology.

8

'A Contented Man'

The oddity of some of Wallace's ideas (on phrenology, on vaccination, on the nationalization of land, and on spiritualism and mesmerism) put him at odds with certain friends and scientific colleagues. To some of the scientific elite of England in the Victorian period, he was an embarrassment. Darwin sometimes despaired; Huxley was on occasion very abrupt. Wallace was also sometimes shy and awkward with others, and this no doubt made him difficult or impossible to employ. This meant, of course, that he was constantly short of funds and so he had to keep his nose to the grindstone writing what would sell (unsurprisingly, scientific papers yielded nothing).

It was impecuniousness, as well as poor judgement, that led him into the flat-Earth fiasco which cost him so dearly in time, worry and money. Throughout his life, he seems to have attracted ill fortune – his father died relatively young, leaving him penniless, and several of his brothers died before their time. An enormous batch of his specimens, and many of his notes, from his South American sojourn went up in flames on the high seas. 'Miss L.', the fiancée with whom he was deeply in love, broke off the engagement and caused him very great pain, upsetting him for many months. This was due to a complete misunderstanding over another female friend, the widow of an Indian Army officer, whom Wallace had no more idea of marrying than 'an aunt or a grandmother'. But, on his own admission, his shyness and difficulty in personal relationships may have contributed to his problems. He survived, however. Darwin wrote a letter to Wallace, now held in the British Library, on 29 January 1865, telling him that hard work was a cure for such misfortunes and disappointments – although this doesn't seem to have helped in the short term.

In due time, however, he found great happiness with Annie. She was the daughter of the botanist Mr William Mitten (an authority on mosses), who lived at Hurstpierpoint in Sussex; Annie was apparently around twenty when he first met her. The courtship was relatively short, and they married in 1866, after which they honeymooned in Wales and later took a longer holiday in Switzerland. 'Five years in quiet enjoyment' (*Life*, II, p 379) of his collections followed.

Nevertheless, Wallace was frequently ill, both while he was in the tropics and after he returned to England – he complained sometimes of asthma and breathlessness when he had to go up and down stairs.

In addition to all this there seems to have been a certain restlessness. Throughout much of his life, Wallace was either travelling, living with relatives or in rented accommodation. In later life, he constantly moved. He sometimes had a logical explanation for his moves – his children's schooling, the local climate, the fact that a property was too far from London and he was therefore constantly having to refuse invitations, the expansion of development nearby – but one might wonder whether his restlessness was simply psychological in character.

Wallace does not seem to have owned a property until he built and lived in The Dell, Grays, Essex from 25 March 1872 to July 1876. This was a large house, designed and built to his specifications, which had 1.5 hectares (4 acres) of land; from this 'picturesque' property, 'there was a beautiful view over . . . to the Kent hills and down a reach of the Thames to Gravesend' (*Life*, II, 91).

Wallace obtained a 99-year lease, said that he hoped to live there for the rest of his life and from May 1872 began to take pleasure in gardening – collecting and growing 'uncommon and interesting', as well as beautiful, plants. He had some assistance but did much of the work himself.

But this residence was to be short-lived; perhaps because of further financial difficulties and the death of his young son, it was sold in July 1876, and for another period of five years, there was constant moving from one rented home to the next. He then built 'a small cottage' at Godalming, Surrey: it had oak trees and hazel bushes in the garden, and he called it 'Nutwood'. Of this property, he wrote,

> The soil was a deep bed of the Lower Greensand formation, with a thin surface layer of leaf-mould, and it was very favourable to many kinds of bulbous plants as well as half-hardy shrubs, several of which grew there more freely and flowered better than in any of my other gardens (*Life*, II, 103–4).

But the oak trees shaded the garden, and Wallace complained that the property was too small. His family moved again, to Corfe View, Parkstone, Dorset, a house with a fine view across to Poole Harbour, the Purbeck Hills and Corfe Castle (hence the name). Here he constructed a pond for waterlilies and other aquatic plants, and also built a special orchid house. Within eight years, however, an expanding Bournemouth had surrounded the property with houses, and Alfred and his wife had to walk a couple of kilometres or so to be in open country. Now they were again on the move, but this time to a site only 6 or 7 kilometres (3½ or 4 mi.) away, where he obtained 1.2 hectares (3 acres) of land, partly woodland, at the end of 1901, and

> began at once making a new garden and shrubbery, decided on plans and began building . . . The main charm of the site was a

Wallace photographed in 1889 by his brother-in-law Thomas Sims.

small neglected orchard with old much-gnarled apple, pear and plum trees . . . In the foreground were clumps of gorse and broom . . . while the orchard was sheltered on both sides by patches of woodland. . . . we got into [the house] at Christmas 1902, when we decided to call it Old Orchard (*Life*, ii, 227).

Fortunately he had retained the Godalming property, having let it out to tenants, and was able to sell it for a good price. This was the tenth move since his return from the Far East. The house was of the 'rambling English country type', on a knoll and with an attractive view of Poole Harbour. Here he gardened, wrote 'six thousand words a day' when he could, played with his children and enjoyed an occasional game of chess with friends and neighbours. Annie helped him with his work, for example in correcting proofs. This last decade of his life was particularly productive. He wrote the following books while living at Old Orchard: *Man's Place in the Universe* (1903, possibly partly written at Corfe View), *My Life* (1905), *Is Mars Habitable?* (1907), *The World of Life* (1910), *Social Environment and Moral Progress* (1913) and *The Revolt of Democracy* (1913). He also edited Richard Spruce's *Notes of a Botanist on the Amazon and Andes* (1908), and in his last eleven years produced about 130 other publications: some of these were very short letters or notes, but they included more substantial pieces. As well as natural history, they dealt with politics, nationalization of the railways, women's suffrage and the possibilities of life on other worlds. If a critical review or comment appeared concerning something he had written, he was quick to reply.

There is something of a *fin de journée* about books in this list. In editing the *Notes of a Botanist*, he was returning to the South America of his youth, the very start of his career in science (Spruce had been with him for a time in South America). In *The World of Life*, we see a summary of Wallace's work in biology, while *Man's Place in the Universe* and *Is Mars Habitable?* see him looking out from this world and speculating on the possibility of life elsewhere in the universe. Admittedly the conception of the absolute size of the universe at that time was a lot smaller than it is now known to be, but on the whole he thought the existence of life elsewhere was unlikely: a supposition that fitted with his teleological views. *Social Environment and Moral Progress* represented an old man's evaluation of the progress (that word again) towards the utopian vision. *My Life*, of course, was his autobiography, looking back on the entirety of his long life and varied experiences. It is detailed, interestingly written and a reasonably honest appraisal, although he is a little

'Old Orchard', near Broadstone, Dorset: Wallace's home from 1902 until his death in 1913, from his autobiography, *My Life* (1905).

selective. His final book was *The Revolt of Democracy* (1913) – we cannot imagine an activist, a protagonist, a polemicist such as Wallace not wanting to have a political last word in his final days, can we?

Some mention has already been made of *The World of Life* and its examples and arguments, but further examination is appropriate here, in the context of it being one of Wallace's final writings. Published three years before he died, it represents a remarkable summary and integration of much of his previous work. Early chapters discuss the distribution of flora and that of animals; he emphasizes adaptation, showing how in both tropical and temperate environments there is evidence of very strong adaptation to environment. The approach is strongly quantitative. He does not use the term 'biodiversity', but he says a great deal about the numbers of species of organism, both plants and animals, in relation to unit area and demonstrates that, as area increases, species diversity increases, but by a smaller proportion. For example, Wallace gives the following data for Macrolepidoptera (butterflies and larger moths) and Coleoptera (beetles):

NUMBER OF INSECT SPECIES IN RELATION TO AREA

	Area in sq. mi.	No. of species – Macrolepidoptera	No. of species – Coleoptera
Great Britain	87,500	822	3,260
County of Essex	1,500	620	1,655
Epping Forest	10	428	Not available

He shows that far greater numbers of plants (or animals) occur per unit area in the tropics than in the temperate latitudes; for example,

TROPICAL FLORAS

Place	Area in sq mi.	No. of species
Malacca	660	2,000
Singapore	206	1,740
Penang	107	1,813
Lagoa Santa, Brazil	66	2,488
Mt Pangerango [Name now given as Pangrango], Java	1.16	1,750
Kambangan Is., Java [Pulau Nusa Kambangan]	1.16	2,400

TEMPERATE FLORAS

Place	Area in sq mi.	No. of species
Mt Nikko [Mt Nikko-Shirane], Japan	360	800
Cape Peninsula, S. Africa	180	1,750
Schaffhausen, Switzerland	114	1,020
Washington, DC	108	922
Hertford (near), UK	80	810
Parramatta River, Sydney	20	620
Capri, Italy	4	719
Edmondsham, Dorset	3	640
Cadney, Lincolnshire	3	720
Thames Ditton	1	400

He uses these data, and others like them, to make a plea for reserves, particularly large ones. He said a great deal about conservation, and the sustainable management of resources, in his later life – it was part of his utopian vision. He pleaded particularly for the conservation of what would now be referred to as the high-biodiversity and high-biological-productivity ecosystems of the tropics. But he always based his opinions on scientific principles. Utopianism was blended with a scientific approach.

Placing the great variety of life on Earth in the context of evolution through natural selection, he argued that an important driver of change and adaptation has been the changing environment of the Earth: earth movement, the rise and fall of sea levels and changes in climate have presented new environments, to which living forms have become adapted. He then goes on to discuss heredity and variation as driving forces for evolution, before looking at changes in the Earth's surface as 'the condition and motive-power for evolution.' He gives a description of the geological column (the sequence of rocks in the Earth's crust) and the evidence for evolution provided by fossils.

He also briefly compared the diversity and complexity of animal and plant communities, past and present, with that of the minute cells that make up the bodies of organisms, and with the complexity of the whole universe, speculating on the reasons for this variety and complexity.

It is here that he would part company with many evolutionists, both his contemporaries and those of today. In some areas of evolution, he stresses, including the development of the human mind and of society, he sees some guiding principle, a trending of evolution towards a goal:

I have fully discussed the evidences in plant and animal life indicating a prevision and definite preparation of the earth for Man – an old doctrine, supposed to be exploded, but which, to all who accept the view that the universe is not a chance product, will I hope, no longer seem to be outside the realm of scientific inquiry.

Still more important is the argument, set forth in some detail showing the absolute necessity of a creative and directive power and mind as exemplified in the wonderful phenomena of growth, of organisation, and fundamentally of cell structure and of life itself.

. . .

[These ideas] I venture to hope, will appeal to some of my readers as the best approximation we are now able to formulate as to the deeper, the more fundamental causes of matter and force, of life and consciousness, and of Man himself . . . destined to a permanent progressive existence in the World of Spirit (*World of Life*, 399–400).

Wallace was a great traveller. And he saw life as a journey – a movement towards a goal. We have noted the teleological nature of much of his thought and intellectual development: he had demonstrated the mechanism whereby life had evolved through geological time. The general sweep of the development of life was from simple to complex – from the simple organisms of ancient seas, through invertebrates towards the vertebrates, and ultimately, as he saw it, to its culmination in humanity. From then on, the direction was towards the development of increased mental, intellectual, moral and social prowess, although he believed that this was probably of a different nature to the 'evolution through natural selection' that had produced the physical human form. From the days of his first acquaintance with Owenism, and his embrace of the aspirations of the mechanics' institutes of the early Victorian period, he had believed in the *improvement* of society, through education and in every other possible way; such was his rationale for opposing vaccination, for advocating the nationalization of land and for the many other campaigns on social issues to which he contributed. In his frequent moving from house to house, was he perhaps consciously or unconsciously on a journey towards the perfect home? He loved beauty, writing lyrical descriptions of birds of paradise and the spectacular butterflies of parts of the Malay Archipelago; he liked flowers, contributing to scientific work on the colours of plants and spending many hours cultivating them in the gardens of the houses in which he lived. His descriptions of these homes often include a mention of their attractive location and the nature of the view.

Maybe, shifting home time and again, searching for an ever more attractive location, and one that best suited his needs and those of his family, was his *progress* towards the goal of perfect home in the perfect location. One suspects that Old Orchard was as close to that perfection, that objective, that he found in his earthly life.

Alfred Russel Wallace in many ways had a difficult life. His formal education was cut short. He lived by selling specimens in his early adulthood, and later from the irregular royalties for his publications, never finding salaried employment. Sometimes he faced real financial difficulties, despite being one of the leading scientists of his age. True, he had faced the rebukes, the pity, the condescension of some of his contemporaries, but the honours that Wallace received were legion. In 1868 he received the Royal Medal of the Royal Society, for which he was nominated by T. H. Huxley. The medal was awarded for 'labours in practical and theoretical zoology'. The Darwin Medal of the Society followed in 1890 – he was the first recipient – granted for 'his independent origination of the theory of the origin of species by natural selection'. He became a Fellow of the Royal Society in 1893. (He had earlier refused the fellowship, but eventually other scientists, including Huxley, persuaded him to accept, which he did, somewhat reluctantly.) He stated that he couldn't understand why he should be honoured in this way, claiming that he had 'done so little of what is usually considered scientific work'. Despite this, he went on to receive the Copley Medal of the Society in 1908; in some respects, this could be considered the ultimate scientific honour.

His contributions to geography were also recognized. In May 1892 he was awarded the Founder's Medal of the Royal Geographical Society 'in recognition of the high geographical value of his great works *The Geographical Distribution of Animals, Island Life* and *The Malay Archipelago*'. In the same month he was awarded the Gold Medal of the Linnean Society (now known as the Linnean Medal). In 1908 this Society – before which his natural selection paper had been read fifty years earlier – presented its gold Darwin-Wallace Medal. (Wallace was the first recipient of this medal, and his was the only gold version ever given.) In 1908 he was also awarded the Order of Merit, the greatest honour that can be given to a civilian by the ruling British monarch: there are never more than 24 living members. It has been described as 'possibly the most prestigious honour one can receive on planet earth' – a *culmination*, perhaps.

Trinity College Dublin bestowed an Honorary Doctorate in 1882 – at that time, the whole of Ireland was part of the United Kingdom. Oxford followed in 1892. Foreign institutions also recognized his distinction: thus in 1870 he received the Gold Medal of the Société de Géographie (Paris). And there were honorary memberships of a host of other foreign, and imperial, scientific societies (including, for example, those of the USA, India, Australia, New Zealand, Austria, the Netherlands, Sweden, Italy and Mexico).

Despite sometimes having lived a life lurching from one financial crisis to another in his earlier days, in his later life he described himself as a contented man. Always extremely modest, and somewhat retiring, in later life he and his friends and family rejoiced in his recognition. Some dignity was finally achieved when, as the result of pressure from Darwin and Huxley, he was awarded a modest government (Civil List) pension of £200 per annum in 1881.

The final decade or so of his life appears to have been happy and serene. He became weaker: when he could not walk far, his gardener trundled him round the garden in a wheelbarrow so that he could see which flowers were in bloom. He sometimes had difficulty with his eyes, and occasional pains in his shoulder, but he remained cheerful: 'Nothing made him happier than some plan for reforming the house, the garden, the kitchen-boiler, or the universe' (obituary notices of Royal Society Fellows). He continued to play chess.

On 1 November 1913, he took a stroll around the garden at Old Orchard. Later in the day he felt weak and shivery. The doctor was called, but the two of them were heard laughing in the study! The following day he felt weaker and did not get up. He became increasingly drowsy and on 7 November he died, aged ninety years and ten months. Wallace was buried in the local cemetery at Broadstone, Dorset. His grave is topped by a fossil tree from nearby Portland. The grave subsequently fell into disrepair, but was restored by a group of devotees in 2000. Two years after his death, however, a memorial plaque was placed in the floor of Westminster Abbey, next to Darwin's and close to those of Herschel, Hooker, Kelvin and Lyell, the greatest scientists of the Victorian period.

9

Some Thoughts on Wallace's Mind and Character

Wallace had a lot to put up with. It was not just that his education was cut short – what he had of it had not been much good, and he was taught subjects that were of little use to him. He was left-handed, but as a youngster was compelled to write with his right hand. The schizophrenic position of pupil-teacher at Hertford unsettled him greatly.

On the other hand, he was blessed with superb powers of observation and an astonishing memory – a memory so good that in the words of one biographer,

> Living to over ninety, he never forgot the details of the anatomy of longicorn beetles, the prerequisites for the brotherhood of man, the best hypotheses to account for strident colours of caterpillars, the tenets of Owenism, or how to make a box with a lid that really fitted.[1]

However, his recollections were sometimes wrong. There are occasional differences in the dates of events between his original notes (and other independent sources) and those given, for example, in *The Malay Archipelago*.

It goes without saying that he was also enormously intelligent. It has, in fact, been said that his lack of formal education helped him, enabling him to see the world in an uncluttered, clear manner, free from intellectual baggage. His uniqueness has also been stressed

– few people, even in the Victorian age, when polymaths were not uncommon, contributed so much in so many fields.

He was unique in his family too. Darwin came from a family of brilliant minds: his grandfather was the scientist and poet Erasmus Darwin (1731–1802); several of his sons were very distinguished in their time, three becoming Fellows of the Royal Society; a grandson, also called Charles (1887–1962), was an FRS and director of the National Physical Laboratory. And the Wedgwood family, with whom the Darwins intermarried several times in three generations, were also extremely accomplished. But there are no figures remotely comparable with Alfred Russel Wallace in his family (although to be fair, it has to be said that that his father and brothers all died much younger than he).

Other Wallace attributes were supreme courage and persistence, almost to the point of foolhardiness. He and H. W. Bates went to South America ill-prepared and with little money, barely into their majority, exploring difficult country, enduring tropical heat in districts prone to disease and surviving enormous hardships and dangers. After losing his specimens in a fire at sea on his way back to England (see Chapter Two), he set off again for eight years of comparable privations in Southeast Asia. He came through it all, although one of his brothers, Herbert, who accompanied him for part of his time in Brazil, died there of yellow fever. But he was also courageous in his published work, for not only did he proselytize for the doctrine of evolution when it was unpopular with many, but his advocacy of ideas such as socialism, the nationalization of land, phrenology and spiritualism brought him scorn and opprobrium in some of the circles in which he desired to move; there is something of an intellectual derring-do about his work that is almost comparable to that of the hardiness he showed during his eleven years of tropical explorations.

Wallace was able to overcome many of the difficulties he faced to a remarkable extent. However, there is some evidence that there

A posthumous portrait of Wallace, attributed to J. W. Beaufort, 1923.

were other aspects that he found challenging for much of his life. In certain circumstances he seems to have lacked empathy and experienced difficulties in dealing with others. The exact nature of the difference that caused Bates and Wallace to part company in South America is not clear: it may have been a disagreement on some trivial matter, although it does seem that the breach was later healed, to some extent. The broken engagement with 'Miss L.'

(Marion Leslie), despite her alleged mistake as to a rival's affections, implies at least some lack of empathy. He almost admits this when, after a year of courtship, Marion refused his advances: 'Evidently my undemonstrative manner had given her no intimation of my intentions.'

His own summary of his character at about this time is telling:

Up to middle age, and especially during the first decade after my return from the East, I was so much disinclined to the society of uncongenial and commonplace people that my natural reserve and coldness of manner, often amounted, I am afraid, to rudeness. I found it impossible, as I have done all my life, to make conversation with such people, or even reply politely to their trivial remarks. I therefore appeared gloomy when I was merely bored. I found it impossible . . . to tolerate fools gladly; while owing to my deficient language facility, talking without having anything to say, was most difficult and disagreeable. Hence I was thought to be proud, conceited or stuck-up (*Life*, ii, 382).

Then there was the absurd incident involving John Hampden, champion of the flat-Earth movement (Chapter Six). Poor naive Wallace saw the challenge as a scientific problem, one to be approached through observation and experiment. Someone less naive would probably have appreciated that anyone who was stridently proselytizing for a 'The Earth is Flat' cause in 1870 is likely to have had some defect in personality at the very least. Perhaps comparable is the enthusiasm with which he testified in court in defence of the charlatan American spiritualist Henry Slade (also Chapter Six).

There are other incidents, too, that speak of his occasional lack of appreciation of society's norms or of the feelings of those around him.

Wallace was . . . inclined to disregard social niceties . . .
[showing] a simple lack of tact. He brought his characteristic
bluntness to even the most exalted of social situations: on
visiting Alfred Tennyson in 1884, he lambasted the House of
Lords and hereditary peerages in general despite Tennyson's
having earlier that year been made a peer.[2]

Even when it was he who was being honoured, he sometimes
showed what some might call a distinct lack of judgement, even
disdain. In 1902 he refused an honorary degree from the University
of Wales – the country of his birth, and to some extent his
formation, for it had been the venue of parts of his early surveying
career – writing to a friend (a Miss Dora Best) of 'The bother, the
ceremony, the having perhaps to get a blue or yellow or scarlet
gown! And at all events new black clothes and a new topper.' He
had earlier declined a similar honour from Cambridge.[3] Perhaps
even more surprising was his refusal to attend Buckingham Palace
for his investiture by King Edward vii into the Order of Merit.

Although he lectured and presented papers to learned societies,
there were times in his life when the thought of public speaking
appalled him:

In the spring of 1890 I lectured at Sheffield and Liverpool,
and have since declined all invitations to lecture, partly from
disinclination, and considerations of health, but also because
I could do more with my pen than with my voice (*Life*, ii, 209).

Probably it was the difficulty he experienced in personal
relationships, perhaps combined with just a touch of arrogance
and one-track-mindedness that prevented his ever obtaining
employment after his early teenage years. The Deputy Secretary
of the Royal Geographical Society was but one of the positions
that he missed. In 1878 he applied for an appointment managing

the 2,250 hectares (5,560 acres) of Epping Forest. In his naivety he rushed into print with an article expressing an extreme conservationist point of view. Vested interests were not impressed and he lost out once more. The only regular work that he was able to undertake was as 'Examiner in Physical Geography under the Science and Art Department'. He undertook this task every year from 1871 until 1897.

Wallace's lack of empathy and intermittent instances of zealotry have led some to suggest that he may have had a correlated group of personality traits and behaviours that are today given the name Autism Spectrum Disorder (ASD) or Asperger's syndrome (a less severe manifestation of autism). The symptoms of this not very well understood psychiatric state include lack of empathy and understanding of others, as well as a preoccupation with a restricted range of topics, sometimes those that are odd or arcane (railway timetables, light switches and mobile phone towers are some modern examples), almost to an obsessive degree. Sometimes this manifests itself in collecting things that may be of little value in themselves. Such persons are also on occasion described as having a compulsive urge to sort or arrange in order the things around them, or to 'build systems'. (For example, some autistic children have a compulsion to arrange their toys in neat rows.) Wallace's almost obsessive desire to collect and own enormous numbers of beetles, and, to a lesser extent, butterflies as well as specimens of other biological groups, including birds and plants, is suggestive here.[4] And from his early perambulations in the Welsh countryside, he seems to have been keen to impose 'order' on his surroundings and collections, constantly wanting to assign a given plant, bird or insect its position in the biological scheme of things.

The extent to which it is useful to pin psychiatric or psychological labels on individuals who are long dead has been subject to a good deal of debate. Such persons are unavailable for testing, and medical and psychological knowledge was very different a hundred, let alone nearly two hundred, years ago. Asperger's syndrome was first discussed by the Austrian physician Hans Asperger (1906–1980) in 1944. Until the 1960s it seems to have been diagnosed very rarely, but the rate of incidence in many Western countries appears to have increased enormously over the last few decades. Whether this reflects a real increase in this mental state in the community, or is a product of greater awareness and more widespread testing, is hotly debated. And whether Asperger's syndrome should be regarded as the manifestation of a real disorder, or whether such persons should simply be regarded as 'different', is also much discussed.[5]

Despite all these uncertainties, the attempt to consider Wallace's characteristics in relation to what are often regarded as symptoms of the condition seems worth making. It should be emphasized that there is a spectrum in the condition: many persons bearing the label are capable of functioning well in society; some are extremely gifted. The possibility that Alfred Russel Wallace was a 'high-functioning' individual who had some of the traits of the syndrome to a certain degree – that he was 'on the spectrum'– should be examined. High intelligence is not incompatible with a position on the spectrum. Certainly one of the main signifiers of the condition is a lack of empathy.

There seems to be some correlation of the syndrome with mathematical ability, although the relationship is not very strong.[6] It is clear that Wallace was quite highly numerate. He rejoiced in utilizing mathematics to real purpose while surveying in Bedfordshire and the Welsh Borders, and he seems to have been quite good at it.[7] His account of an interview for a school-teaching post in 1844 is also instructive:

> The [school] required, in addition to English, junior Latin and algebra. Though I had not looked at a Latin book since I left school, I thought I might possibly manage; and as to algebra, I could do simple equations, and had once been able to do

quadratics, and felt sure I could keep ahead of beginners. So with some trepidation I went to interview the master, a rather grave but kindly clergyman. I told him my position, and what I had been doing since I left school. He asked me if I could translate Virgil, at which I hesitated, but told him I had been through most of it at school. So he brought out the book and gave me a passage to translate, which, of course, I was quite unable to do properly. Then he set me a simple equation, which I worked [out] easily (*Life*, I, 229–30).

He seems to have picked up quite a bit of mathematics while teaching in Leicester. The headmaster, a Mr Abraham Hill, was 'a high Cambridge wrangler' and finding Wallace 'was desirous of learning a little more algebra offered to assist me. He lent me Hind's algebra which I worked through successfully.' This gave Alfred an interest in mathematics which he 'never lost'.

Although he claimed to have no great ability in the subject, throughout his scientific career he used numerical evidence whenever it seemed to him appropriate. He was among the first to use a quantitative approach to biogeography: his books are full of tables comparing the numbers of species in particular categories in different areas – for example, those that were east and west of 'Wallace's Line' (see Chapter Five). He went through the Registrar General's statistics with a fine-toothed comb in his (misguided) attempt to demonize vaccination, producing elaborate graphs in an attempt to illustrate his points. It has to be said, however, that there are occasional errors in his calculations! Both mathematical ability and the incidence of Asperger's syndrome/autism spectrum disorder appear to be higher in males (the ratio of males to females for Asperger's syndrome is about 4:1).

Such individuals are described as good at sorting, or placing things in order, and from his early youth, when identifying plants and assigning them to their families, Wallace seems to have excelled in this. He later became more and more involved in the classification of organisms. Many of his papers were on taxonomy and nomenclature: of plants, birds, butterflies and moths, and beetles. This can be seen as fulfilling an urge to impose order on nature and to 'systematize'.

Collecting can also be interpreted as a way to impose order (see also Chapter Five). Again, the urge 'to have and to hold' appears to be more common in males than females. Wallace had this drive to collect to a high degree: from the time he met Bates while he was teaching at the Collegiate School in Leicester, he was an inveterate collector. Birds, butterflies, moths and beetles were especially favoured while he was in the Malay Archipelago, and besides acquiring tens of thousands of specimens for sale to collectors and museums in Europe, he accumulated a massive personal collection, which he used for research. While from time to time he applied for salaried positions, he was not altogether upset when he failed to obtain appointments: they would have failed to allow him time to attend to his collections! (See also Chapter Five.)

When his specimens were lost in the fire on his way back from South America, he was annoyed at the loss of those he might have sold, but his greatest regret was that the richest part of his *private* collection had also disappeared:

> The hundreds of new and beautiful species [of insects and birds] . . . *would have rendered (I fondly hoped) my cabinet, as far as regards American species, one of the finest in Europe.* (emphasis added: *Life*, 1, 305.)

In later life, the collecting of living plants for his gardens seems to have taken over to some extent from the accumulation of dead insects.

Collecting and categorizing or pigeon-holing go together. And some folk have a real ability in the latter, for example naturalists with an 'extraordinary on-board natural database', partly based on memory and partly on the ability to classify or order. Andrew Berry, in his essay hinting at the possibility that Wallace was 'on the spectrum' emphasized that two of the most eminent modern evolutionary biologists and students of evolution – Ernst Mayr (1904–2005) and Edward O. Wilson (1929–) – show amazing abilities in identification and taxonomy in particular groups of organisms. Mayr's special skill was in the identification of birds, and Wilson had 'one of those extraordinary on-board databases, one that allows him to identify at a glance any species of *Pheidole*, a vast taxonomically diverse group [of ants] containing over 625 described species.'[8] To some extent at least, good naturalists are born rather than made, having a special combination of mental abilities.

It is often stated that persons with autism spectrum disorder have a good eye for detail. This would be logical, bearing in mind their abilities in classification and sorting, and would certainly fit with what is known about Wallace: he could, for example, recognize very minor differences in the wings of butterflies (see Chapter Three). He loved facts and was at great pains to record them. A couple of Cambridge researchers referred to system-building (systematizing) as follows in 2006:

In contrast to these difficulties [in social interaction, empathy], individuals with A.S.C. [autism spectrum conditions, which include Asperger's syndrome] show good and sometimes even superior skills in 'systemising' . . . Systemising is the drive to analyse or build systems, to understand and predict the behaviour of . . . events in terms of underlying rules and regularities. Individuals with A.S.C. are hyperattentive to detail and prefer predictable, rule-based environments, features that are intrinsic to systematizing. In addition, individuals with A.S.C. are superior to controls on various tasks that involve searching for detail, analysing and manipulating systems.[9]

Although there is no suggestion that Wallace was near the severe end of this disorder, he certainly did have an eye for detail and was undoubtedly good at system building, to the extent that he could integrate information from different sources – for example, the habitat, appearance and behaviour of an organism – to build up a coherent picture (see Chapter Three). He was able to assemble his model of natural selection by showing the relationships between a series of facts: the propensity for numbers to increase (as demonstrated by Malthus); the checking of population growth through predation, and so on; the natural variation of organisms; competition (the battle for survival); and the effect of heredity (which, of course, he did not fully understand) – an example of system-building if ever there was one!

Recently, attempts have been made to show that a number of distinguished scientists were 'on the autism spectrum'. Ioan James, the distinguished Oxford mathematician, suggested that this diagnosis might apply to Sir Isaac Newton, Henry Cavendish and Albert Einstein.[10]

Alfred Russel Wallace had a number of characteristics that were not advantageous to him – socially and certainly financially. His naivety seems to have led to some disastrous investments (a characteristic he appears to have shared with his father). It could also be argued that his naivety led him astray when he was entranced by the odd and unconventional, such as spiritualism and phrenology. And yet . . . and yet . . .

Just possibly, his being 'on the spectrum' – albeit in a position where he was often able to function reasonably well (he claimed his 'organ of language' was poor but gave lectures and coped with travel and instructing employees in remote regions) – may have had advantages. His numeracy, his 'system-building' ability, his extraordinary eye for detail and his collecting imperative were all characteristics that helped to mark him out as a superb naturalist and brilliant theorizer. His willingness to break with convention,

Antony Smith's 2013 statue of Wallace as a 'bug-hunter' outside London's Natural History Museum.

to risk annoying people, put him in the forefront of the large cohort of explorer-naturalists of the nineteenth century, and ultimately made him, in old age, an honoured and contented man. Hans Asperger himself is quoted as follows:

> It seems that for success in science or art a dash of autism is essential. For success the necessary ingredient may be an ability to turn away from the everyday world, from the simple practical, an ability to rethink a subject with originality so as to create in new untrodden ways, with all abilities canalized into the one speciality.[11]

Out of the deep depths of misfortune comes bliss. (Anon)

Chronology

1823   Born Llanbadoc, near Usk, Monmouthshire, Wales.

1828   Family moves to Hertford; education at home and at Hertford Grammar School. Works as 'pupil-teacher' in his final year.

1837   Works briefly in London for a small master-builder. Attends Hall of Science; reads widely on secularism and Owenism. Works with his elder brother William, beginning his training as a land-surveyor in Bedfordshire.

1839   Works briefly for a watch-maker in Leighton Buzzard. Later travels to Kington, Herefordshire with his brother William, working as a surveyor in the Welsh Borders. Associated with Kington Mechanics' Hall.

1841   Moves to Neath, Glamorgan. Reads widely in science, particularly geology and botany.

1844   Finds work teaching at the Collegiate School, Leicester. Meets H. W. Bates; becomes interested in entomology, particularly the collecting of beetles.

1846   Elder brother William dies. Alfred returns to Neath to wind up the surveying business. Associated with Neath Philosophical and Literary Institution.

1847   Corresponds with Bates about 'the species question'. Prepares for trip to South America.

1848   Sails to South America on the *Mischief*.

1848–52 Extensive travel in South America; collects thousands of natural history specimens. Publishes several scientific papers.

1852   Returns to England on the *Helen*. Fire destroys the ship and almost all of Wallace's specimens.

1852–4 Lives in England on proceeds of insurance payout for destroyed specimens; meets British naturalists; addresses scientific institutions; writes extensively.

1854   Arrives in Singapore.

1854–62 Extensive travel and collecting of natural history specimens throughout the Malay Archipelago. Interested in variation and distribution of organisms. Financially supported though the sale of specimens.

1858   The 'natural selection' insight. Later this year, joint presentation of Wallace's paper and certain writings of Charles Darwin to the Linnean Society in London by Charles Lyell and Joseph Hooker.

1859   Publication of *On the Origin of Species by Means of Natural Selection* by Charles Darwin.

1862   Returns to England.

1862–5 Lives in various places in south and southeast England; lectures and writes extensively. Broken engagement with Marion Leslie.

1866   Marries Annie Mitten.

1869   Publishes *The Malay Archipelago*, dedicated to Charles Darwin.

1870	Involvement with John Hampden – 'the flat-Earth incident' caused worry and financial loss for many years.
1876	Publishes *The Geographical Distribution of Animals*.
1881	Awarded Civil List Pension of £200 per annum.
1882	Awarded Honorary Doctorate by Trinity College Dublin.
1886–7	Tour of the USA.
1889	Publishes *Darwinism*.
1892	Founder's Medal of the Royal Geographical Society
1902	Final house move, to Old Orchard, Dorset.
1903	Publishes *Man's Place in the Universe*.
1905	Publishes autobiography: *My Life*.
1907	Publishes *Is Mars Habitable?*
1908	Awarded a gold Darwin-Wallace Medal from the Linnean Society. Awarded Order of Merit by King Edward VII.
1910	Publishes *The World of Life*.
1913	Dies at Old Orchard; buried at Broadstone, Dorset.
1915	Memorial plaque placed in Westminster Abbey, close to those of Darwin, Herschel, Hooker, Kelvin and Lyell.

References

1 Early Life

1 This fact is perhaps worthy of note, as there is some evidence that children born later have a tendency to be 'the rebel of the family'. See F. J. Sulloway, *Born to Rebel: Birth Order, Family Dynamics, and Creative Lives* (New York, 1996); P. A. Rohde, F. J. Sulloway et al., 'Perceived Parental Favoritism, Closeness to Kin and the Rebel of the Family: The Effects of Birth Order and Sex', *Evolution and Human Behavior*, 24 (2003), pp. 261–76. As the title of the latter implies, this matter is one of some complexity.

2 In 1800 Robert Owen had become part-owner and manager of the New Lanark cotton mills in Scotland. There he established a social welfare programme, building a 'model community'.

3 Belemnites are the bullet-like fossil remains of an extinct form of cephalopod, somewhat similar to squid. They are not uncommon in the Mesozoic rocks of eastern England.

4 Almost certainly *An Account of the Operations Carried Out for Accomplishing a Trigonometrial Survey of England and Wales*, by Captain William Mudge, FRS, and Mr Isaac Darby (London, 1799). William probably owned a later edition.

5 Two decades later, mechanics' halls were sufficiently part of the English townscape to figure in popular songs. Geordie Ridley's 'Blaydon Races' – the unofficial Tyneside anthem – was written in 1862. One verse runs,

> We flew across the Chain Bridge right into Blaydon town,
> The bellman he was callin' there, they call him Jackie Brown;
> I saw him talkin' to some chaps, and them he was pursuadin'
> To go an' see Geordie Ridley's concert in the Mechanics' Hall at Blaydon.

6 Parts were published in R. Elwyn Hughes, 'Alfred Russel Wallace: Some Notes on the Welsh Connection', *British Journal for the History of Science*, 22 (1989), pp. 401–18.

7 Stanner Rocks are quite close to Kington, although just in Wales. In fact, they consist of gabbro, granite and diorite, rather than basalt. With an age of about 700 million years, they are among the oldest in Wales.

8 Dietrichsen and Hannay's *Royal Almanack and Nautical and Astronomical Ephemeris*. It is a publication produced each year, giving astronomical tables along with other topical information.

9 Authorship by Scottish journalist Robert Chambers (1802–1871) was revealed in the twelfth edition, published in 1884. *Vestiges* was a strange, philosophical work that contained much that scientists found absurd. Thomas Huxley, later evolution's champion, savaged it in what has been described as 'one of the most venomous reviews ever written'. Nevertheless Chambers saw the evolution of plants and animals as a steady, upward progress governed by ascertainable natural laws.

10 William had travelled to London to give evidence on the South Wales Railway Bill, and returning to South Wales in an open, third-class carriage, had caught a severe cold, which later caused 'congestion of the lungs'. Alfred railed against the evils of poverty, and the distasteful task of collecting small debts due to William's estate from those reluctant to pay was perhaps one factor that encouraged him to leave Britain.

11 *Zoologist*, 5 (1847), p. 1676.

12 The bulk of the short unattributed quotations in this chapter are from volume 1 of A. R. Wallace's autobiography *My Life* (1905).

2 South American Journey

1 W. H. Edwards, *A Voyage up the River Amazon, Including a Residence at Pará* (London, 1861), pp. 28–9 (original edition, New York, 1847).

2 Quoted by James Marchant in *Alfred Russel Wallace: Letters and Reminiscences* (London, 1916), p. 92.

3 Note the repetition of the words 'facts' and 'collection', two preoccupations of Wallace's throughout his career.

4 A. R. Wallace, 'On the Umbrella Bird (*Cephalopterus ornatus*)', *Proceedings of the Zoological Society of London*, 18 (1850), pp. 206–7.

5   A. R. Wallace, 'Journey to Explore the Natural History of the Amazon River (extracts from letters dated 15 Nov. 1849, Santarem, and 20 March 1850, Barra de Rio Negro, to Samuel Stevens [Wallace's agent, responsible for the sale of specimens collected])', *Annals and Magazine of Natural History* (series 2), VI/36 (December 1850), pp. 494–6.

6   A. R. Wallace, 'On the Monkeys of the Amazon', *Annals and Magazine of Natural History*, 14 (1854), pp. 451–2.

7   Ibid.

8   A. R. Wallace, 'On the Habits of the Butterflies of the Amazon Valley', *Transactions of the Entomological Society of London* (new series), II/8 (1854), pp. 253–64.

9   A. R. Wallace, letter dated 19 October 1852, *Zoologist*, X/119, pp. 3641–3.

10 The majority of the short unattributed quotations in the chapter came from volume I of Wallace's autobiography, *My Life* (1905).

3 Eight Years in Southeast Asia

1   A. R. Wallace, 'On the Habits of the Butterflies of the Amazon Valley', *Transactions of the Entomological Society of London* (new series), II/8 (1854), pp. 253–64.

2   Ibid.

3   Amabel Williams-Ellis, *Darwin's Moon: A Biography of Alfred Russel Wallace* (London and Glasgow, 1966), pp. 83–4, quoting Royal Geographical Society Papers.

4   Linnean Society of London Archives.

5   Gambir = *Uncaria gambir*. A plant formerly widely grown in Southeast Asia for its use as a herbal medicine and in tanning.

6   We may note that the population of the now highly urbanized Singapore was 2.618 million in 2015.

7   Letter reproduced in *Zoologist*, XV/179 (1857), pp. 5652–7.

8   Letter held by Natural History Museum.

9   E. O. Wilson, *Sociobiology: The New Synthesis* (Cambridge, MA, 1975), pp. 331–5.

10 It should be noted that the first edition of *The Malay Archipelago* appeared in 1869, ten years after the publication of *On the Origin*, although before the appearance of *The Descent of Man* in 1871. It is

uncertain to what extent Wallace thought about an evolutionary link between the apes and humanity while in Southeast Asia.

11 Letter to his boyhood friend, George Silk, 22 December 1861, in *Alfred Russel Wallace: Letters from the Malay Archipelago*, ed. J. van Wyhe and K. Rookmaaker (Oxford, 2013), p. 275.

12 Large, mound-building birds: genus *Megapodius*.

13 The majority of the short unattributed quotations in this chapter come from *The Malay Archipelago*.

4 The Natural Selection Insight and Its Aftermath

1 *Transactions of the Entomological Society of London*, IV/7 (1858), pp. 272–3.

2 *Zoologist*, XVI/185–6 (1858), pp. 5887–8. Wallace was, however, an almost obsessive collector – it was his livelihood – so he must have examined hundreds of specimens of many species. John van Wyhe in *Dispelling the Darkness* (Singapore, 2013, p. 186) has suggested that the variations he noted in tiger beetles he had collected in Macassar in about November 1857, which were coloured exactly like the shiny brown mud on the edge of a creek, were important in developing Wallace's thinking. He had previously found others resembling 'the white sand of Sarawak' and the 'dark sand' of Bali, and Van Wyhe tentatively suggested that Wallace's tiger beetles were his 'equivalent of Darwin's legendary finches'.

3 *Correspondence of Charles Darwin* (CCD), ed. F. Burkhardt and S. Smith, vol. VI (Cambridge, 1990), p. 387.

4 *Journal of the Proceedings of the Linnean Society of London: Zoology*, 3 (1859), pp 45–62.

5 Ibid., p. 45.

6 Letter dated 25 January 1859 from Charles Darwin to A. R. Wallace. Original in British Library: CCD, vol. VII, pp. 240–41.

7 Quoted in Michael Shermer, *In Darwin's Shadow: The Life and Science of Alfred Russel Wallace* (Oxford, 2002), p. 144.

8 'The big species book', written between 1856 and 1858, was not published until 1975, under the title *Charles Darwin's Natural Selection*, ed. R. C. Staffer (Cambridge).

5 The Maturing Scientist

1 Letter from Wallace to Bates, quoted in A. Berry, '"Ardent Beetle-hunters": Natural History, Collecting, and the Theory of Evolution', in *Natural Selection and Beyond: The Intellectual Legacy of Alfred Russel Wallace*, ed. C. H. Smith and G. Beccaloni (Oxford, 2008), p. 55.
2 Letter from Wallace to Edward Newman, 9 May 1854, from Singapore, in *Alfred Russel Wallace: Letters from the Malay Archipelago*, ed. J. van Wyhe and K. Rookmaaker (Oxford, 2013), p. 16.
3 Letter from Wallace to George Silk, 20 January 1862, from Singapore, ibid., p. 277.
4 A. R. Wallace, 'On the Phenomena of Variation and Geographical Distribution as Illustrated by the Papilionidæ of the Malayan Region', *Transactions of the Linnean Society of London*, xxv/1 (1865), pp. 1–71, plates 1–8.
5 'On the Physical Geography of the Malay Archipelago', *Journal of the Royal Geographical Society*, xxxiii (1863), pp. 217–34.
6 Ibid.
7 Quoted in J. Marchant, *A. R. Wallace: Letters and Reminiscences, Pt ii* (London, 1916).
8 A. R. Wallace, 'Caterpillars and Birds', *The Field, the Country Gentleman's Newspaper*, xxix/742 (1867), p. 206.

6 The Radical and the Heretic

1 Letter, A.R.W. to George Silk, 22 December–20 January 1862, *Alfred Russel Wallace: Letters from the Malay Archipelago*, ed. J. van Wyhe and K. Rookmaaker (Oxford, 2013), pp. 276–7.
2 M. Shermer, *In Darwin's Shadow: The Life and Science of Alfred Russel Wallace* (Oxford, 2002), p. 242.
3 A. R. Wallace, 'The Origin of Human Races and the Antiquity of Man Deduced from the Theory of "Natural Selection"', *Journal of the Anthropological Society of London*, 2 (1864), pp. clviii–clxx.
4 A. R. Wallace, *Land Nationalisation Society – Tract 3: How Land Nationalisation Will Benefit Householders, Labourers and Mechanics* (no date, probably about 1882).

5 There is some evidence that Gladstone may have seen a copy of the earlier (1885) pamphlet. A copy is held by Gladstone's Library, Hawarden, North Wales. It is among the books originally owned by this prime minister and is lightly annotated, possibly in his hand.

6 Some jurisdictions, while not making immunizations compulsory, impose sanctions upon those who do not co-operate. Thus Australia does not provide family assistance payments to families with unimmunized children. Some countries do not allow attendance at public (that is, state) schools.

7 A. R. Wallace, 'Glacial Epochs and Warm Polar Climates', *Quarterly Review*, CXLVIII/295 (1879), pp. 119–35. Wallace, 'The Ice Age and Its Work', *Fortnightly Review*, 54 (1893), pp. 616–33, 750–74.

8 A comparison may perhaps be made with the ideas of Taillard de Chardin.

9 J. Moore, 'Wallace in Wonderland', in *Natural Selection and Beyond: The Intellectual Legacy of Alfred Russel Wallace*, ed. C. H. Smith and G. Beccaloni (Oxford, 2008), pp. 353–67.

7 To the End of the Universe

1 A. R. Wallace, 'On the Physical Geography of the Malay Archipelago', *Journal of the Royal Geographical Society*, 33 (1863), pp. 217–34.

2 A. R. Wallace, 'Epping Forest', *Fortnightly Review*, 24 (1878), pp. 628–45.

3 See Chapter Three.

4 A. R. Wallace, 'Man's Place in the Universe', *Independent* (New York), LV/2830 (26 February 1903), pp. 473–83.

5 A. R. Wallace, *Man's Place in the Universe: A Study of Scientific Research in Relation to the Unity or Plurality of Worlds* (London, 1903), pp. v–vi.

6 The existence of any canal-like features was completely disproved in the 1960s and early 1970s by NASA's *Mariner* missions, which found no evidence of canals but revealed a much-cratered Martian surface. Today, the markings taken as canals are assumed to have been an optical illusion.

7 Wallace, *Man's Place in the Universe*, pp. 314–15.

8 Ibid., 2nd edn (1904), Appendix, pp. 334–5.

9 Some Thoughts on Wallace's Mind and Character

1 Amabel Williams-Ellis, *Darwin's Moon* (London, 1966), p. 231.
2 A. Berry, ed., *Infinite Tropics: An Alfred Russel Wallace Anthology* (London, 2003), p. 382.
3 A. Marchant, *Alfred Russel Wallace: Letters and Remembrances*, vol. II (London, 1916), p. 222.
4 A. Berry, '"Ardent Beetle-hunters": Natural History, Collecting, and the Theory of Evolution', in *Natural Selection and Beyond: The Intellectual Legacy of Alfred Russel Wallace*, ed. C. H. Smith and G. Beccaloni (Oxford, 2008), pp. 47–65. This source was particularly useful in compiling this chapter.
5 A useful source on the diagnosis and treatment of people with autism and Asperger's syndrome is T. Attwood, *The Complete Guide to Asperger's Syndrome* (London, 2008). Use was also made of ICD-10 (the 10th revision of the International Statistical Classification of Diseases and Related Health Problems/Classification of Mental and Behavioural Disorders), a medical classification list produced by the World Health Organization (Geneva).
6 S. Baron-Cohen, 'Mathematical Talent is Linked to Autism', *Human Nature*, 18 (2007), pp. 125–31.
7 Surveying would appear to be an excellent example of 'system building' or 'systematizing': see below.
8 See Berry, '"Ardent Beetle-hunters"', pp. 47–65.
9 O. Golan and S. Baron-Cohen, 'Systemizing Empathy: Teaching Adults with Asperger Syndrome or High-functioning Autism to Recognize Complex Emotions Using Interactive Multimedia', *Development and Psychopathology*, 18 (2006), pp. 591–617. S. Baron-Cohen also discusses male–female psychological differences in *The Essential Difference: The Truth about the Male and Female Brain* (Reading, MA, 2003).
10 Ioan James, FRS, 'Singular Scientists', *Journal of the Royal Society of Medicine*, XCVI/1 (2003), pp. 367–9.
11 Hans Asperger, 'Formen des Autismus bei Kindern' [Forms of autism in children], *Deutsches Arttzeblatt*, XIV/4 (1974).

Select Bibliography

By A. R. Wallace

The most important books written by Alfred Russel Wallace include the following:

My Life: A Record of Events and Opinions, vol. I (London, 1905)
My Life: A Record of Events and Opinions, vol. II (London, 1905)

The Malay Archipelago: The Land of the Orang-utan and the Bird of Paradise.
A Narrative of Travel with Studies of Man and Nature (London, 1869).
There have been many subsequent editions of this work, including
The Annotated Malay Archipelago, ed. J. van Wyhe (Singapore, 2015)

The Geographical Distribution of Animals; with a Study of the Relations of
Living and Extinct Faunas as Elucidating the Past Changes of the Earth's
Surface (London, 1876)

Darwinism (London, 1889)

The Wonderful Century: Its Successes and Its Failures (London, 1898)

Most of the above, along with the majority of Wallace's other publications, are available online at 'Wallace Online', see http://wallace-online.org

Other Works

The following are significant biographical and critical works on Wallace, and anthologies of his work:

Berry, A., ed., *Infinite Tropics: An Alfred Russel Wallace Anthology* (London and New York, 2002)

Fichman, M. *Alfred Russel Wallace* (Boston, 1981)

Shermer, M., *In Darwin's Shadow: The Life and Science of Alfred Russel Wallace* (Oxford and New York, 2002)

Smith, C. H., and Beccaloni, G., eds, *Natural Selection and Beyond: The Intellectual Legacy of Alfred Russel Wallace* (Oxford, 2008)

Van Wyhe, J., and K. Rookmaaker, eds, *Alfred Russel Wallace: Letters from the Malay Archipelago* (Oxford, 2013)

Van Wyhe, J., *Dispelling the Darkness: Voyage to the Malay Archipelago and the Discovery of Evolution by Wallace and Darwin* (Singapore, 2013)

Williams-Ellis, A., *Darwin's Moon: A Biography of Alfred Russel Wallace* (London and Glasgow, 1966)

Acknowledgements

I acknowledge, with grateful thanks, the support of Peter Francis, warden of Gladstone's Library, Hawarden, Flintshire, North Wales. Gladstone's Library (formerly St Deiniol's) is the ideal environment for research on, and writing about, nineteenth-century thought. The link is particularly appropriate because the life of the statesman and the naturalist Wallace overlapped for some 75 years, and their lives were intertwined at a couple of junctures. I thank also the late Professor Bob Keegan (to whose memory this book is dedicated); Bruna Bekle, who read parts of the text; and my dear wife Moyra, whose love and support never failed however long I was immersed in the machinations of nineteenth-century science, religion and politics.

The assistance of the Reid Library of the University of Western Australia, and the Australian National Library in the provision of illustrative material is also acknowledged.

Photo Acknowledgements

The author and publishers wish to express their thanks to the below sources of illustrative material and/or permission to reproduce it.

From Henry Walter Bates, *The Naturalist on the River Amazons: A Record of the Adventures, Habits of Animals, Sketches of Brazilian and Indian Life, and Aspects of Nature under the Equator, during Eleven Years of Travel*, 2 vols (London, 1863): pp. 34, 38, 50 (vol. I) and p. 39 (vol. II); from *Borderland: A Quarterly Review and Index*, III/2 (April 1896): p. 134; from Pieter Cramer, *De Uitlandsche Kapellen: voorkomende in de drie Waereld-Deelen Asia, Africa en America . . . Papillons Exotiques des Trois Parties du Monde, l'Asie, l'Afrique et l'Amerique . . .* (Amsterdam, 1775–82): p. 74; from G[eorgiana] Houghton, *Chronicles of the Photographs of Spiritual Beings and Phenomena Invisible to the Material Eye* (London, 1882): p. 123; from the *Journal of the Royal Geographical Society*, vol. XXXIII (8 June 1863): p. 93; from W.H.G. [William Henry Giles] Kingston, *Shipwrecks and Disasters at Sea* (London, 1875): p. 45 (image kindly provided by the Australian National Library, Canberra); from Percival Lowell, *Mars* (Boston, MA, and New York, 1895): p. 133; Natural History Museum, London: pp. 150, 159; from Alfred Russel Wallace, *The Malay Archipelago: The Land of the Orang-utan, and the Bird of Paradise. A Narrative of Travel, with Studies of Man and Nature*, 2 vols (London: 1869): pp. 55, 64, 86, 91 (vol. I) and pp. 60, 62, 75 (vol. II); from Alfred Russel Wallace, *My Life: A Record of Events and Opinions*, 2 vols (London, 1905): pp. 10, 12, 33, 52, 125 (vol. I) and pp. 99, 124, 141 (vol. II); photo Wellcome Images: p. 10.

The Wellcome Collection, the copyright holder of the images on pp. 25, 51, 69, 78, 81, 82, 119 and 139, have published them online under conditions